The Cruise of the I

Ralph Stock

Alpha Editions

This edition published in 2022

ISBN : 9789356151543

Design and Setting By
Alpha Editions
www.alphaedis.com
Email – info@alphaedis.com

CHAPTER I

On dreams, and the means to realize them

We all have our dreams. Without them we should be clods. It is in our dreams that we accomplish the impossible; the rich man dumps his load of responsibility and lives in a log shack on a mountain top, the poor man becomes rich, the stay-at-home travels, the wanderer finds an abiding place.

For more years than I like to recall my dream has been to cruise through the South Sea Islands in my own ship, and if you had ever been to the South Sea Islands, it would be yours also. They are the sole remaining spot on this earth that is not infested with big-game-shooting expeditions, globe-trotters, or profiteers, where the inhabitants know how to live, and where the unfortunate from distant and turbulent lands can still find interest, enjoyment, and peace.

My dream was as impracticable as most. There was a war to be attended to and lived through if Providence so willed. There was a ship to be bought, fitted out, and provisioned on a bank balance that would fill the modern cat's-meat-man with contempt. There were the little matters of cramming into a chronically unmathematical head sufficient knowledge of navigation to steer such a ship across the world when she *was* bought, and of finding a crew that would work her without hope of monetary reward.

The thing looked and sounded sufficiently like comic opera to deter me from mentioning it to any but a select few, and *they* laughed. Yet such is the driving power of a dream if its fulfilment is sufficiently desired that I write in retrospect with my vision a secure and accomplished fact.

Exactly how it all came about I find it difficult to recall. I have vague recollections of crouching in dug-outs in France, and while others had recourse during their leisure to letter-cases replete with photographs of fluffy girls, I pored with equal interest over plans and designs of my dream ship.

In hospital it was the same, and when a medical board politely ushered me into the street a free man, it took me rather less than four hours to reach the nearest seaport and commence a search that covered the best part of six months.

It is no easy matter to find the counterpart of a dream ship, but in the end I found her patiently awaiting me in a backwater of glorious Devon:—a Norwegian-built auxiliary cutter of twenty-three tons register, designed as a lifeboat for the North Sea fishing fleet, forty-seven feet over all, fifteen feet beam, eight feet draught, built to stand up to anything, and be handled by a crew of three or less. Such was my dream ship in cold print. In reality, and seen through her owner's eyes, she was, naturally, the most wonderful thing that ever happened. A mother on the subject of her child is almost derogatory compared with an owner concerning his ship, so the reader shall be spared further details.

Having found her, there was the little matter of paying for her. I had no money. I have never had any money, but that is a detail that should never be allowed to stand in the way of a really desirable dream. It was necessary to make some. How? By conducting a stubborn offensive on the Army Authorities for my war gratuity. By sitting up to all hours in a moth-eaten dressing-gown and a microscopic flat writing short stories. By assiduously cultivating maiden aunts. By coercion. By—— But I refuse to say more.

The dream ship became mine, but what of a crew? Well, I have a sister, and a sister is an uncommonly handy thing to have, provided she is of the right variety. Mine happens to be, for she agreed to forego all the delicacies of the season and float with me on a piece of wood to the South Sea Islands. So also did a recently demobilized officer who, on hearing that these same islands were not less than three thousand miles from the nearest early-morning parade, offered his services with almost unbecoming alacrity.

With ship and crew accounted for, those unacquainted with the intricacies of ocean cruising may imagine there was nothing more to be done than to sail. Others, who have perhaps trodden the thorny path leading to the fulfilment of a dream such as ours, will realize that our troubles had little more than begun. The hull of a ship—even a dream ship—is a thing vastly different from a vessel fully equipped for a voyage. The difference between a house "furnished" and "unfurnished" is nothing to it. We needed an auxiliary motor engine for entering and leaving port if we would escape extortionate towage charges. We needed copper sheathing to protect our future home against the dreaded cobra worm of tropical waters that has been known to reduce sound wood to the semblance of a honeycomb within six months. We needed water tanks to contain three hundred gallons, oil tanks to hold two hundred, nautical instruments and gear of every possible description, not to mention provisions for an indefinite period.

Exactly how we were to acquire these things without the proverbial penny to do it with was a problem that gave us pause until at an extraordinary, general meeting of the firm of Peter, Steve, and Myself, dream merchants, it was proposed, seconded, and carried unanimously that we suffered from lack of capital, and that, in the words of the chairman, we should have to scatter and scratch for it.

So, each to his method!

Peter became what is called in the advertisements "useful maid" to an exacting invalid of religious and parsimonious tendencies at a South Coast resort. Steve faded into the smoke of a great city on a mission the details of which he has never divulged to this day, though judging by its success I am divided in my surmise as to its nature between "bridge" and robbery with violence.

As for me, I saw nothing for it but a return to the moth-eaten dressing-gown—until I happened to visit the local fish market and asked the price of sole. The answer caused me furiously to think. There were a hundred and fifty sailing vessels in this old-fashioned Devonshire fishing fleet, each earning a handsome income, and not one of them a better craft than mine. Why not go trawling with the dream ship?

This I did, and propose to give a brief account of my experiences for the benefit of those desirous of knowing one way of making a ship pay for herself.

From frequent recourse to the bar-parlour of "The Hole in the Wall," a far-famed hostelry replete with smoke-grimed rafters and sawdust floor, I learnt that the universal custom amongst fishing craft thereabouts was to have a crew of three: two "hands" and a skipper. The money that the catch of fish realized on sale by auction was divided at the week end into five, a share each for the crew, and the remainder going "to the ship" or, in other words, to the owner, who is responsible for all gear.

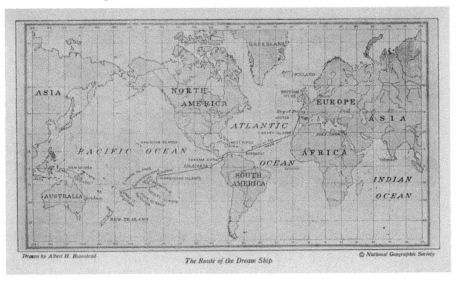

The Route of the Dream Ship

As regards nets: there are two kinds of trawl net, the "beam" and the otter. Imagine a huge, meshed jelly-bag being towed along the bottom of the sea, and you have the net. But how is the mouth of it, which is often twenty feet long, kept open? In the case of the beam trawl, by a wooden spar terminating each end in iron "heads"; and this is the usual type of net for the sailing smacks comprising the main fleet. But for smaller craft, such as motor boats, a beam trawl is too heavy and unwieldy; consequently the otter trawl was invented.

Ready for Sea · Photo by Ralph Stock

Ready for Sea

This consists of two boards about three feet by four, weighted at the bottom, and attached to each corner of the mouth of the net. They are "slung" at such an angle that the force of the water as the boat tows them along the bottom of the sea forces them outward, like kites, and thus keeps the mouth of the net stretched. In addition to this, the top of the net's mouth is kept up by cork, and the bottom down, by leads disposed along the foot-rope. It is a simple contrivance, like most things ingenious.

Ninety fathoms of warp, and two wire "bridles," one leading to each board, and thirty fathoms in length, complete the fishing gear, which is paid out and hauled in by means of a hand capstan.

All these articles I somehow acquired, including a "hand" of forbidding aspect, and a boy. The dream ship was converted into a smack with as much expediency as an elderly shipwright with a taste for beer, and his accomplice, a lad of fifteen, allowed; and finally she stood, a thing of such beauty in smacks that I wrote a sonnet to her, which shows the appalling effects of freedom, sea air, and a fish diet.

My opinion of her, however, was not shared by the fishing fraternity. Almost everything that could be wrong with a smack was the matter with the dream ship according to these chronically pessimistic gentry. She had too much freeboard. She had too much beam for her length. Her bulwarks were not high enough. She would never "tow" (trawl).

Yet upon a never-to-be-forgotten morning we sailed—dearly beloved word of infinite possibilities!—we sailed at a seven-knot clip for precisely ten miles. We could beat the ketch-rigged smacks of the fleet to wind'ard without topsail or staysail. I grinned, the boy grinned, even the "hand" grinned as he looked aloft; and it was at that precise moment that I saw his grin fade into an open-mouthed, wide-eyed stare.

"She's gone at the eyes of the rigging," was all he said, with complete composure, and in rich Devonian.

We put about. The mast-head was leaning at an angle of forty degrees, and wabbling on its splintered base like a drunken man. The "hand," in white chin whiskers, enormous boots, and a bowler hat dented on one side, continued to grin. In that hour I hated the man. To him it was a gigantic joke, an amusing problem as to whether we could reach harbour before the mast fell about our ears. To me, the owner of a dream ship, it was tragedy. There are moments when even a sense of humour can be out of place.

One hundred yards from our moorings the mast "went" at the deck as well as the hounds, and fell with a crash the full length of the ship—without touching a soul. It was little short of a miracle, and for a few moments we stood in our several places pondering it.

The mast had scarce met the deck, with the sails and rigging hanging over the side in a tangled mass, when a smack's crew was alongside. Did we want help? We did, but hardly expected such a stiff bill for salvage as was rendered the next day.

It took three weeks to step the dream ship's new mast; three miserable weeks of waiting that only those who have "fitted out" can appreciate. But in time we sailed afresh. We even launched the trawl with much shouting and flurry, and at the end of two hours' speculation hauled it up again by sheer brawn and the capstan, got the net aboard, and found mud, nothing but mud, in the cod-end.

Various explanations were forthcoming from the "hand" for this calamity. There was too much lead on the foot-rope. There was too much cork on the head-line. The otter boards were not slung true. We had been towing too fast. We had been towing too slow. Why, bless your heart, there were men (successful fishermen now) who had spent months in adjusting an otter trawl. An inch this way or that made all the difference. An otter trawl was like a watch. Out of all this the hard fact emerged that we had caught no fish.

Fisherman

For two weeks we were out early and late experimenting, and for two weeks I scraped together (Heaven knows how!) sufficient for the "hand's" retainer and my own board and lodging. And then—success came to us as by a miracle. Instead of mud, or shells, or weed, we found fish in the cod-end: fat plaice, luxurious sole, skate, and whiting.

What we had done to our otter trawl I don't think anyone knew, least of all the "hand," and I am none the wiser to this day, but it caught fish. We treasured that trawl as something exceedingly precious, and nothing, nothing whatsoever, would cause us to alter its ropes or leads a hair's breadth. We lived in constant dread that we should meet a "hitch" (an obstacle on the bottom of the sea) that would make it necessary to cut the warp and lose this wonderful trawl. It would have taken two weeks, perhaps two months, to discover another like it, and we were averaging fifty pounds a week.

Success breeds ambition, and I installed a motor auxiliary engine. Further, there is only one way of catching more fish than by trawling all day, and that is trawling all night. The fish, especially whiting, do not see the net coming in the dark. So we acquired the habits of night-hawks, sailing at four o'clock in the afternoon, and returning at six the next morning. It paid. It paid handsomely. What should I not be able to report at the next general meeting of dream merchants?

It was a fine sight on a pitch-black night to see our wake streaming away like smoke from the propeller, so bright with phosphorescence that it seemed a powerful light must be hung over the stern. And to watch the net, lit with a myriad tiny lamps, creeping in yard by yard. Then, what a splashing as the big skate and plaice came alongside!

It must be remembered that the dream ship's career as a fishing smack was during the last phases of the great war. She saw three German submarines, two steamers sunk, and had her stalwart ribs severely shaken by depth-charges on several occasions. In fact, as one concussion caused her to leak, I had serious thoughts of decorating her with a wound-stripe on the starboard quarter. What the effect of one of those fearful implements of destruction must be at close quarters, and while submerged, I can hardly imagine. I only know that one was dropped about half a mile from the dream ship, and from the cabin it sounded as though someone had hit the oil-tanks with a sledge-hammer, and felt as though she had run bow on, and at a nine-knot clip, into an iceberg.

Over twenty good, sound fishing smacks belonging to the fleet with which we sailed were sent to the bottom by German submarines. In one case the crew were stripped of their jerseys—the only article aboard the smack that seemed to appeal to the Hun—and left on deck while the submarine submerged under their feet. The one survivor's chief complaint appeared to be the loss of his jersey.

On more than one occasion a German submarine appeared in the midst of the fishing fleet, which they favoured as an unsuspected lurking-place. Warps were cut on the instant, and, under full sail, a hundred smacks might have been seen racing harbourward minus their gear. This became such a common occurrence that patrol boats were sent out with the fleet, and "forbidden areas" created.

These last were unpopular with fishermen. The authorities seemed to pitch inevitably on the most prolific grounds to place under the ban. Poaching became general. In one instance the skipper of a smack, who had had a bad "week's work," decided to make amends or perish in the effort. He altered the registered number of his boat, which is carried in large white figures on the mainsail and bow, with whitewash, burnt-corked the faces of himself and his crew, and sailed for the banned area.

For hours he trawled backward and forward across the holy ground, with dread and hope alternating in his heart, and with the first hint of dawn hauled in his net, to discover that in the general excitement he had "shot" his trawl with the cod-end untied!

Nothing daunted, he returned to the attack the following night, and as Fate the Jester so often decrees, on this occasion, when the cod-end was securely tied and all going well, the hated voice of the fisheries inspector, better known as the "bogey-man," came out of the night, close alongside: "You are reported for trawling in the proscribed area."

Simultaneously a shaft of light from an electric torch bit into the darkness, exposing the smack's number and her black-faced crew.

"Stand by. I'm coming aboard," were the next instructions, but the men were suddenly electrified into life. In stony silence, so that their voices should not be recognized, the skipper successfully threatened the boarding "bogey-man" with a cutlass, while the crew set the steam capstan to work and soon had the trawl aboard with its valuable freight.

With the "bogey-man" still threatening dire vengeance, the smack stood out to sea, and catching the morning breeze, outstripped the inspector's launch. The authorities never knew who perpetrated this outrage, as, when they came to look up the smack's number in the register, they found it to be that of an antiquated hulk that had never left harbour.

It is to be feared that the dream ship poached. On one occasion a thick fog descended upon her while trawling. She continued the motion blindly for three hours, when the fog lifted and we discovered—naturally with deep regrets—that we had covered a forbidden area from end to end, and had caught sole, plaice, and turbot to the value of forty pounds.

The dream ship had many experiences while "paying for herself," and was destined to have many more. For her size, it is doubtful if any craft has enjoyed a more varied life, and the more I think of her lying there in foreign waters, ... But of this anon.

THE PREPARATION

Concerning preparations in general, and personnel in particular

CHAPTER II

Concerning preparations in general, and personnel in
particular

Our separate excursions into the field of commerce resulted in a healthier financial outlook at the next general meeting of dream merchants. Plans developed apace. Lists were made, schedules drawn up. An actual sailing date began to emerge out of a welter of conjecture.

On paper, the dream ship was converted from a work-worn fishing-smack into a cruiser yacht of comfort and elegance within a month, and a trifle under the estimated cost.

On paper, the art of navigation was acquired in our spare time, after the airy fashion of a Correspondence-School advertisement.

And again on paper—a map of the world outspread on the cabin table, to be exact—we actually decided on our route. At the point of an indomitable lead pencil we traversed vast tracts of ocean in the winking of an eye, and explored the furthermost corners of the earth; and if there is a more fascinating evening's entertainment, I should like to hear of it.

Spain should be touched at, for the sake of her wine, if nothing else; perhaps Madeira, and most certainly the Canary Islands. After that, there was the little matter of the Atlantic Ocean, ending in the West Indies. Then came the Caribbean Sea, the Panama Canal, and so down into the milky way of the Pacific. It looked a long way; it *was* a long way, but we had a ship, and we had a crew, and what was the sea if not the highway of the earth? The enthusiasm of ignorance? Perhaps; yet I am convinced that without the enthusiasm, and most certainly without the ignorance, we should never have set sail, much less won through to our goal.

The transition from fancy to fact was effected the following morning, when Steve and I commenced the soul-racking task of transferring twelve tons of rusty pig-iron from the dream ship's bilge to the quay alongside which we lay. This mass of obstinate metal had to be chipped and painted, and ultimately replaced so that we might disport ourselves on our beam ends, if the elements so willed, without shifting it. It was one of the dream ship's strong points, that her ballast was all "inside." There was no "fin" of lead hanging from her keel, that might come adrift from a multitude of causes, and leave us a tottering hulk. I told Steve this, as we wrestled with two hundredweight pigs, that had a knack of slipping their moorings in mid-air, and crashing through the cabin floor boards, or on to our anatomies with striking impartiality. I told it to him again, as we sat in the rain on the quay, chipping rust into each other's eyes, but received no satisfactory reply on either occasion.

"By the way," was all he said that evening, when, weary and bruised and rusty, we flung ourselves on our bunks, "according to schedule, this is where we study navigation, isn't it?" And for three mortal hours he gave his undivided attention to a nautical epitome. That is the kind of man Steve is.

There is no undertaking that requires a more careful selection of personnel than a cruise such as we contemplated, and no better opportunity of taking a man's measure than when fitting out! By the time it is done, one has either come to the conclusion that the other fellow has his points, or that to remain in his company another hour is beyond endurance. Naturally, his feelings are similar, and that we of the dream ship stood the mutual test seemed to me to augur well for the future.

It was during this trying period that we encountered a peculiarly pernicious type of the genus yachtsman on his native heath. He was owner of a pretty little six-tonner across the creek, and was "fitting out" also—had been for two months, as far as we could gather. The thing was evidently a hobby with him that he infinitely preferred to getting to sea. With a paint pot in one hand, and a camel's hair brush in the other, he advanced on his craft in the manner of an artist attacking a master canvas, applied the pigment, and stood back with his head at an angle to view the effect. In itself there was nothing against this form of amusement, provided that it interfered with no one else; but, evidently tiring of his own company, at which I am not surprised, our yachtsman strolled in the direction of the dream ship to offer unsolicited criticism.

Photo by Ralph Stock
The Reciprocal Morning Douche, Mid-ocean

Photo by Ralph Stock
Steve at the Sextant and Peter at the Helm

The Reciprocal Morning Douche, Mid-ocean;
Steve at the Sextant and Peter at the Helm

"Fine craft you have there," was his introductory remark, and my heart warmed to him. Here, at all events, was a judge. "But too much beam for her length, and too much *flaire*. She'll break your heart going to wind'ard," he added, judicially, and I confess to loathing him on the instant. Imagine a stranger approaching you in the street and saying: "Fine wife you have there, but I don't like her face—or her action." Well, that is how I felt. For you must be told, unless you are an "owner" and know already, that the simile of the ship and the wife is not so far-fetched as may appear. Yet, with superhuman restraint, I continued to chip iron while it was pointed out to me that lead was better, that to paint spars instead of varnishing them was a crime, and to paint decks was worse; in short, that most things about the dream ship met with this yachtsman's hearty disapproval. To which I was constrained to make answer that with all her defects the dream ship happened to satisfy *me* because I was an ex-fisherman and not a yachtsman; that for one thing I could not afford to be a yachtsman, and for another I had no wish to be a yachtsman, being rather too fond of the sea. So we parted the best of enemies, and had not done with each other, as will transpire later.

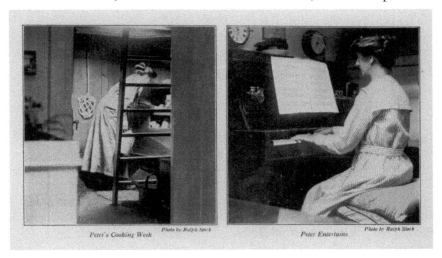

Peter's Cooking Week   Photo by Ralph Stock   Peter Entertains   Photo by Ralph Stock

Peter's Cooking Week;
Peter Entertains

The moral of this somewhat hectic interlude is: when fitting out for a cruise, get the advice of a deep-water man, and find a place where there are no yachtsmen. This last is difficult, but it is worth while.

Much the same thing applies to the study of navigation. If the beginner lends an ear to the horde of amateur cranks who dabble in the subject, and who seem obsessed with a desire to impart their half-baked theories to others, he will know as much about the practical business of finding a ship's position at sea as he does about the origin of life. There is the long lean man, usually with a drooping moustache, who demonstrates on an instrument of his own invention that can do anything but talk—this last deficiency being amply atoned for by the inventor himself. There is the man with "short cuts" and "clean cuts." There is even the man who still persists in the belief that the world is "flat with rounded edges," and produces reams of his own screed, printed at enormous expense, in support of his theories; but he is easily disposed of. After admitting that the shape of the world is not a burning question with you anyway, because after all it is not a bad old world and certainly the best we can expect in this life, you confess to a sneaking suspicion that it is a rhomboid.

No, there is only one way of learning to find a ship's position at sea if you are unable to spend three months or more at a school of navigation, and that is to find a retired master mariner who, for a stipulated sum, will teach you exactly what he did himself probably three hundred and sixty-five times in the year for thirty years. Hearken unto him, in spite of all lures to the contrary, and in three weeks or less the miracle will cease to be a miracle.

We of the dream ship were fortunate in running such a mentor to earth in his charming cottage on the hillside, overlooking the harbour. The Skipper, as he shall henceforth be called, was of the old school, and so, if it is permissible to say such things of a lady, was his wife! This remarkable woman followed the sea with her husband on every ocean-going schooner he commanded, and once, when the entire crew was down with beri-beri, and a voracious tug hovered alongside like a bird of prey, she brought the ship to port single-handed, thus saving the owners a stupendous sum for salvage. They rewarded her with a presentation piano, and she wept. She could not play. So a cheque for a hundred guineas was substituted, and her husband alleges that she bought three new hats and a galley range in which she cooks the acme in figgy dough to this day.

Using a sextant

The Skipper, a man of monumental and very necessary patience, received us each day in a torture chamber of his own, replete with thumb screw and rack in the form of nautical epitomes, and model craft at variance on the placid surface of a deal table. That small room was the scene of strange and tragic happenings. Gales, fogs, collisions, lee shores, and shipwreck followed one another in rapid succession, and invariably terminated in the short, sharp query: "What do you do now?"

But these things constituted seamanship, which is essentially a matter of experience, not of rote. It was after our first, second, and even third day of attempting to find longitude that we reeled from the classroom, our heads a whirling chaos of logarithms, traverse tables, and despair. At no time that I can recall did our dream come so near to dissolution.

"Have you," muttered Steve, as we paused during our descent to the town, and the strongest cup of tea procurable, "have you the foggiest idea of what we are driving at?"

I admitted that I had not, and the funereal procession proceeded on its way.

There are two methods of attacking the problem of navigation: one is by intelligent understanding, and the other by rule of thumb. If yours is the type of mind that revels in mathematics, then the first is obviously your course, and a pleasant one at that. If, upon the other hand, you are cursed, as I am, with a mind that reels at the mere sight of a timetable, then the second has its points, for you get there just the same, and in spite of experts' warnings to the contrary. Without knowing the why or wherefore of your figurative acrobatics, provided you follow the rule of thumb implicitly, and can add, subtract, multiply, and divide correctly, there is nothing to prevent you from finding a ship's position at sea day in and day out, identically with the greatest experts on earth. I have done it, and I have a shrewd suspicion, backed by the opinion of the Skipper, that more than one master mariner does it in precisely the same way. All hail to logarithms, and the obscure but miraculous gentleman who invented them!

At long last there came a day when the shipwright's hammer ceased to resound aboard the dream ship, and save for provisions and water, and a snowdrift of unpaid bills, we were ready to take leave of the yards.

With an ebb tide and the faithful Skipper aboard, we dropped down the river, and as cleanly as may be on to a mud bank! I am not going to say how it happened, because I do not know. All we were acutely conscious of at the time was that our yachtsman, in his pretty little six-tonner, had chosen the same date of departure as ourselves, and was rapidly approaching down the channel that we should have followed, and had not, and that somehow the secret of our dream must have reached his protruding ears, for as he came abreast of us he reared his hideous form out of the cockpit.

"Hullo," he cried. "Have you made your South Sea Islands already?"

We did not answer, there was nothing to be said; but when a tug hauled us free on the next tide, and rounding a bend in the river, we came upon our adversary in precisely the same predicament, we passed him in silence, the most satisfying silence I have ever indulged in.

Without a dissentient voice, the task of choosing and stowing the provisions was relegated to Peter——— "A woman is so much better at that sort of thing." Steve and I admitted as much, with touching magnanimity.

In due course a cart backed up to the quayside, and an active little grocer proceeded to heap the dream ship's deck with comestibles—tinned, boxed, and jarred. These we passed through the skylights, before an admiring audience of fisher-folk, and Peter, being ambidextrous, contrived to stow them in the lockers with one hand and make a list of them with the other.

I have my own notions about provisioning a dream ship in the future—if for me there is a future in dream ships. During the following year we proved, to our own dissatisfaction, that although tinned food is mighty handy, it is not a healthy continuous diet... No, I see myself laying in salt junk of the windjammer variety, plenty of waterglassed eggs and condensed milk, good ship's biscuits, a "crock" of hand-salted butter, dried fruits, jam or marmalade to taste, pickled beetroot for the blood, flour, raisins, and baking powder, Scotch oatmeal, sugar, tea, coffee, cocoa, and lard, and nothing else whatsoever. It may be asked: "What else could there possibly be?"—to which I make answer: "A hundred and one canned atrocities, such as Somebody's curried giblets, or Somebody Else's evaporated tripe, that it were better if one consigned to the deep than ate." It is extraordinary the number of useless things one can be lured into acquiring while "fitting out," and we of the dream ship bought most of them.

"Barter" was Peter's idea. In her mind the word was inalienably associated with the South Sea Islands, and were we not bound thither? It was only another example of her boundless optimism. Steve and I might furtively discuss the number of miles between ourselves and our goal, the probable discomfitures by the way, even the possibility of not getting there at all. Not so Peter. We were going to the South Sea Islands, and to go to the South Sea Islands without "barter" was a thing undreamed of in her philosophy. Hence a hurried pilgrimage to London, and the purchase, out of our rapidly diminishing capital, of variegated prints, looking-glasses, imitation tortoise-shell hair combs, Jew's harps, and brown paper belts.

On our return, the Skipper, who had remained aboard as watchman during our absence, displayed a certain uneasiness, the cause of which was hard to determine. He expressed his keen admiration for the dream ship, as he had often done before, and then paused, until goaded into the confession that he wished he thought as much of her crew. That is not how he put it, but that was what he meant, and we were inclined to agree with him. In other words, it was on the dear old man's conscience that he was letting us go to sea with insufficient knowledge, a scruple as rare as it is refreshing these days. We immediately and unanimously pointed out that there was only one way out of the dilemma, and that was for him to accompany us. He shook his grizzled head, and smiled wistfully; said it was twenty years since he had been to sea, that he was too old, that his "missus" would never let him go, and finally, with a twinkle in his keen blue eye, that he would come as far as Spain "just to get us into the hang of longitude," whereat we fell upon him in a pæan of gratitude.

Behold, then, the crew of the dream ship ready to sail, with a combined capital of one hundred pounds sterling, and a clearance for Brisbane, Australia.

AT VIGO, OFF THE COAST OF SPAIN

Some confessions and a few morals

CHAPTER III

Some confessions and a few morals

At six o'clock the next morning a small, depressed-looking procession wended its way to the quay, followed by the sidelong glances and whispered comments of the fish-market fraternity.

It was the noble army of dream merchants setting forth on its quest. And why depressed? I do not know, except that, personally, on the eve of any problematical undertaking I feel that way, and so, apparently, do others. Perhaps it was that the enthusiasm of ignorance had momentarily deserted us, and we were awed by a rational glimpse of the task that lay ahead. Such moods vanish the instant one gets down to work, the great panacea, but until then they crouch on the shoulders, a dour company.

In silence we rowed out to the dream ship, and hoisted sail. I was going to say that in silence we lowered the dinghy on to its chocks, but, as a fact, the keel descended on the Skipper's toe, extracting a shout of anguish from that usually restrained mariner.

Almost simultaneously, and for no apparent reason, Steve took an involuntary seat on the open skylight, which shut with a crash on one of his fingers.

The moorings were cast off prematurely, and, getting under way on the wrong tack, we sailed, with the utmost precision, into a neighbouring fishing-smack, nearly breaking our bowsprit.

I could imagine the grinning heads of the fisher folk lining the breakwater wall.

"They be goin' ter the South Sea Islands, they be!" I could almost hear them saying, and dived below to show them what a motor auxiliary could do. There were one hundred and fifty vessels moored in that harbour, and I should not like to say how many we fouled during the next half hour. Indeed I could not, for throughout the process I was wrestling with the engine, which refused to budge—until we had rounded the breakwater, and there was no further use for it. Such is the way of these necessary evils aboard a sailing ship.

Coming on deck, I was confronted with a sorry spectacle. Our port light-board was in splinters. Relics of vessels we had caressed in parting littered the deck. The Skipper was in the steering well, with the tiller in one hand and his toe in the other; and Peter was administering iodine and lint to Steve's crushed finger.

"She goes!" I triumphed, tactlessly referring to my Herculean labours with the engine.

"D'you think it's broken?" demanded the Skipper, extending an enormous, bootless foot.

"Flat as a pancake," muttered Steve.

Which gives a fair idea of the trend of individual thought on occasions.

But at long last we were off! Off before a seven-knot nor'-wester, and with only twelve thousand miles to go! What else mattered?

Sailboat, flying fish

By the time we had picked up an intermittent pallor on the horizon that was Ushant light at a distance of thirty miles, the wind had strengthened to half a gale, and there was nothing the dream ship loved more dearly than half a gale on the quarter. In a series of exhilarating swoops, it flung her down into the Bay of Biscay; but what she did not like was being left there to roll helplessly in a windless swell. I have to call it a "swell," just as I have to say we "rolled," though neither word conveys our subsequent acrobatics in the least.

"The Bay" has an unsavoury reputation anyway, but for sheer unpleasantness commend me to the mood in which the dream ship made its acquaintance.

Literally from beam end to beam end we lurched. The engine was useless. Our propeller was out of the quarter, and under present circumstances as much out of the water as in it.

Any one aboard capable of sea-sickness, promptly *was*. The Skipper who, it must be confessed, had not been able to eat since setting sail, though he clung to his duties like a Stoic, was as near plaintive as I have ever seen him. Curiously enough, his malady took the form of conjuring visions of his good wife's cooking. I honestly believe that if we had been able to produce the roast beef, cabbage, and "figgy dough" of his own home table, he would have eaten. But all we could offer him was bovril, tongue, and tinned asparagus. We did not know how to live, he assured us. On the schooner in the old days he had a *stove*, not one of these newfangled tin contraptions. And his wife cooked. And when she cooked, she *cooked!* Figgy dough that melted in the mouth.

At this juncture his audience was well advised to move to a safe distance.

In response to our eternal lurchings, ominous sounds began to filter up from below. A metallic click-clock, click-clock, a methodical thudding, a resounding crash. The first of these proved to be a kerosene tank that had come adrift from its rack fastenings, and threatened to fall on the engine. A galvanized iron receptacle containing seventy gallons of liquid is not the easiest of things to handle in a seaway, let alone with a crushed finger. My heart went out to Steve, but it was characteristic of the man that never a whimper escaped him. All that we could do was to wedge the tank into place with stout battens clean across the ship, which we did, and turned our attention to the next calamity. The piano had followed the example of the tank, and the wash-hand stand had emulated the piano; and rather than appear peculiar, a two-hundred-pound drum of treasured Scotch oatmeal was rolling on the floor, mingling its contents with the brine that oozed from a crate of salt pork wedged under the cabin table.

The crash was merely the dethronement of a lighted stove in the fo'c's'le, on which Peter had been persisting for the last hour, and in spite of her own condition, in an attempt to produce something that the Skipper *would* eat.

On the whole, a healthy lesson in making all secure before sailing.

In the midst of our agonies below, a stentorian voice hailed us from the cockpit:

"All hands on deck! Lower mainsail!" Which was followed almost immediately by a "crack" like a pistol shot.

Our boom had snapped clean off about five feet from the end.

Such is "the Bay" in lightsome mood. Apparently the only article aboard unaffected by it was the chronometer, ticking placidly in its gimbals and bed of plush. There was something enviable about that chronometer.

The dawn brought with it a faint but steady breath, and discovering that there was sufficient boom left to set a double-reefed mainsail, we continued on our way, and a blessedly even keel, until toward evening we raised the coast of Spain.

The welcome and unmistakable smell of land came to us over the water, and presently the mouth of the Vigo River opened out, revealing a maze of leading lights.

The engine behaved itself, and by midnight the dream ship had anchored off the town, to an accompaniment of star shells and crackers.

It pleased us to imagine that these were our welcome, but as a fact the inevitable Spanish fiesta was in progress. We had made our first foreign port.

THE CANARY ISLANDS

Dropping the pilot—and the result

CHAPTER IV

Dropping the pilot—and the result

Our first and imperative need was sleep. There comes a time when enforced wakefulness causes the eyes to feel as though they were sinking into the head. We of the dream ship had reached this pitch, and turned in "all standing," to remain log-like until disturbed by port officials at five o'clock the next morning.

In a state of pyjamas and semi-torpor I handed them the ship's papers, which proved to be satisfactory; Steve treated them to a few chosen words in near-Spanish picked up during a doubtful past in Mexico, and we tumbled in again. But not to sleep. Thereafter, an endless procession of boats, manned by picturesque and voluble brigands who offered for sale every conceivable commodity from anchor chain to picture postcards, succeeded in dragging us from our bunks, and propelling us on deck.

A pleasant little town is Vigo. One of a goodly number scattered over the world that I should like to make my home. Each to his taste, and perhaps I am impressionable as to the desirable spots of this earth, but to my way of thinking almost any race knows how to enjoy life better than the Anglo-Saxon of to-day, and fashions its surroundings to that end.

From the river front, with its handsome promenade, hotels, and green, open spaces, Vigo climbs the sunny hillside in cheerful fashion. No one seems overburdened with business cares, but when such things have to be attended to, the palm-fringed *Alamada* takes the place of an office, and the "deal" is discussed over *vino tinto* and cigarettes, to the accompaniment of an excellent band.

We of the dream ship went ashore with the Skipper wearing a fancy-worked carpet-slipper on one foot and a boot on the other, but no one appeared to notice the peculiarity, and it is quite certain the Skipper would not have minded if they had. His is a type of hardihood that I envy as much as I admire.

At lunch, too, he found cause for complaint in the food, and small wonder. After a week's enforced abstention, he found that in these benighted parts figgy dough was as unprocurable as elsewhere. Frankly, he was disappointed in Vigo and, after limping over the cobblestones in clothes more adapted to the Arctic than to Spanish sunshine, he returned aboard "to do a few jobs." We knew what this meant. He would systematically and efficiently set right everything that was wrong aboard the dream ship—a long-splice here, a bit of carpentry there—which was precisely what we ought to have been doing instead of gallivanting about Vigo. Most excellent of skippers! He had been a tower of strength to us in time of stress, and a qualm seized me when I secured his passage to Southampton, and realized that in another week he would be gone.

From the quaint cobbled and terraced streets of the old town we went down to the *Alamada*, and sat for a while watching the children dance to the music of the band. No organized, mechanical spectacle this, but a joyous affair of rhythmic abandon, twinkling legs, and laughter. Most of us like to think that the children of our own particular country are the most desirable, and they would be poor folk who did not; but for unconscious grace of movement and dainty appearance, the Spanish kiddy is hard to beat.

And this happy absence of self-consciousness is not confined to the children. Picture, if you can, and as we of the dream ship saw him a little later, a well-dressed Spanish gentleman standing in the middle of one of Vigo's main thoroughfares and gazing toward the housetops, apparently engaged in practising the deaf-and-dumb alphabet. No one of the stream of pedestrians passing along the sidewalks took the slightest notice of him. Neither did the wheeled traffic, except to swerve obligingly out of his path. It was *his* affair, and a love affair at that. He was conversing with his *enamorata* at the third-floor balcony window in the only way possible to a suitor in Spain, where parents firmly believe in "love at a distance" until the actual engagement. And it needed three vulgar sightseers such as the crew of the dream ship to find anything unusual in the proceeding. I am ashamed to say that the lady caught sight of us, and pointed in alarm, whereat the gentleman turned with an excusable frown of annoyance, and we hurried on our way.

There are only two things the Spaniard takes really seriously: his love and his bull-fights. Leave him to them, as you value a whole skin.

Our next introduction was to the local cable office. Personally, I have always regarded such places as drab receptacles for grudging messages, but with the Eastern Telegraph Company it is a different matter. Certainly this admirable concern takes your message, but then proceeds to take you to its heart, and thereafter, wherever its myriad wires extend, you may be sure of a welcome from the kindliest of hosts. It conducts you to its palatial bachelor quarters situated on the hillside behind the town, and proceeds to spoil you with every device known to a pampered age. Tennis, golf, dances, and dinners are yours to repletion, followed by moonlight car rides into the country, and feasts at distant *fondas* under the trellised vines.

At any rate, that is what it did with us, and we tried to reciprocate. The Eastern Telegraph Company, or as much of it as could get aboard at one time, made the dream ship its headquarters during our stay; dived from her bowsprit or under her keel with equal delight, mealed off strange messes in her seething saloon, and sang songs on deck to Peter's piano accompaniment below.

With such distractions afoot, it is small wonder that nearly a week slipped by before the subject of a sailing date received the attention it deserved. The Skipper grunted his disapproval of our dilatory methods, and pointed out in a satirical fashion peculiarly his own that there were "things" to be done. Amongst them, he mentioned the necessity of making out a new deviation card by the Polar Star, whereat Steve and I collapsed. Had we not done with this pest of deviation? Had we not already discovered and tabulated, at the cost of terrific mental effort, the error of the dream ship's compass owing to local attraction?

The Skipper admitted as much with a wistful smile, but pointed out that deviation has an aggravating habit of changing with latitude. It was the first we had heard of it, and that night we sat again under our long-suffering professor, and swung the dream ship to a mocking North Star.

Island

Then there was the matter of our broken boom. The Skipper and I towed it over, neatly scarfed (dovetailed and bound) from a neighbouring shipyard the next morning. And the instability of things below as demonstrated in the Bay of Biscay? This was remedied by having iron bands placed round everything movable, and screwed to bulkhead or floor. We were ready. The Skipper stepped ashore with his modest little suitcase, and limped away without so much as a backward glance. Why? His "missus" has told me since that he never expected to see us again.

So we three and the dream ship dropped down Vigo River bound for Las Palmas, Canary Islands, with the biggest mixed cargo of hope and ignorance that ever put to sea.

Four hours on and eight off was how we apportioned our watches and, thanks to fair winds and the easy handling of the dream ship, it was seldom necessary for more than one of us to be on deck at a time. In fact, there were hours on end when the helmsman could peg the tiller and take a constitutional.

Cooking we took week and week about, a dreaded ordeal. It is one thing to concoct food in a porcelain-fitted kitchen on *terra firma*, and quite another to do it over a primus stove in a leaping, gyrating fo'c's'le. Porridge was found adhering to the ceiling after Steve's "week," but hush! perhaps he may have something to say on the subject of Peter and myself. There is always plenty to say about the other fellow, but in nine cases out of ten it is best left unsaid. Forbearance is as much the keynote of good-fellowship on a dream ship as elsewhere—perhaps more—and we are rather proud of the fact that we have covered half the world without battle, murder, or sudden death.

With only three of a crew some of our troubles may be imagined, but undoubtedly the worst of these, after a couple of weeks at sea, was being awakened from a trance-like sleep to take a trick at the tiller. One does not feel human under such circumstances, but more in the nature of a bear disturbed during hibernation.

And the awakener's task is not much better. He is forced to peg the tiller, even with a following wind, nip below to resuscitate somehow his log-like relief, and get back before the ship jibes. If there is time he may employ the proper and humane method of applying gradually increased pressure to the sleeper's arm until he awakes. If there is not, he must resort to any merciless method that proves effective. In either case, he is as unpopular as an alarm clock, which, by the way, we tried, but discarded on account of its waking everyone aboard.

The manner of our several wakings formed an interesting, if somewhat intimate, subject of discussion at breakfast one morning. Peter's was voted uninteresting because whatever means were employed to arouse her she merely opened her eyes, and meekly murmured: "All right." Steve, upon the other hand, was uncertain. If he happened to be dreaming at the time, which was usually the case, he either hit out the instant he was touched, or muttered something unintelligible, and tenderly covered the disturbing hand with his own.

As for me, I yawned cavernously, invariably said: "How's she going?" and almost as invariably fell asleep again. Or so runs the report, and one is not permitted to argue with reports. Verily, if man would discover himself—and others—let him have recourse to a dream ship and a crew of three!

It was during the passage from Vigo to Las Palmas that we first experienced that most aggravating of winds, the light, varying, following. I have heard schooner skippers declare that they prefer the "head" variety, and I can well believe it. At night, when it is exceedingly difficult to tell where such a wind is coming from, it is no more pleasant to jibe inadvertently than to have to do so sometimes thrice within the hour to keep the ship on her course. It wears out a short-handed, light-weight crew (Peter turned the scale at ninety-eight pounds, Steve at one hundred and forty-five, and myself at one hundred and forty), and conservation of energy, which makes for good health, is of prime importance on a voyage such as ours.

Finally, we lowered the mainsail, with its jolting, crashing boom, and carried on in blessed tranquillity under a squaresail, which proved to be the most useful sail we had aboard.

At the end of seven days' routine, and fair but light winds, we experienced the acute joy of finding land precisely where our frenzied calculations had placed it. As Madeira loomed on the starboard bow, Steve was seen to pace the deck with a quiet but new-born dignity—until hailed below to help wash dishes. But even this failed to quell the navigator's exuberance, and the dish-washer exchanged views on the subject with the helmsman through the skylight. This, then, was the navigation that master mariners made such a song and dance about! Well, we must be master mariners, that was all we had to say! We had summoned Madeira, and Madeira had appeared! We were not at all sure that we had not discovered Madeira!

Peter seemed strangely unimpressed. Perhaps she sensed what is indeed a fact, that luck in navigation, as in most things, favours the beginner. For instance, a mistake somewhere in our calculations brought us as near disaster in the next twenty-four hours as one cares to be. Taking Madeira as our point of departure, we shaped a course for Las Palmas, giving the intervening Salvage Islands a berth of ten miles to the westward. We reckoned this a safe distance, considering that according to "sailing directions" there was still more to the westward a strong current inclining toward the African coast. Well, that current failed to register in the particular case of the dream ship, and on top of it the "mistake somewhere" caused a cold shiver to traverse the spine of the helmsman when, at one o'clock of a pitch-black night, while doing a comfortable seven knots, a mass of rock reared itself out of the sea seemingly not more than a few hundred yards, though probably more nearly a mile, to starboard.

It was the westernmost island of the Salvages, uninhabited, unlighted, and this same helmsman who, as it happens, was myself, would like to know what prevented the "mistake somewhere" from being just that trifle bigger necessary to land us in splinters on the rocks, the fate of more than one good ship provided with a lookout and master mariner. Surely the luck of the beginner!

The incident gave us violently to think, and we thought again when, a few days later, on summoning the island of Grand Canary with the magic wand of sextant and logarithm, it failed to materialize. Had we overrun the entire Canary Group, and were we gaily heading for the African coast with its picturesque Riff pirates who specialize in becalmed ships, or were we even now heading for the iron-bound coast of Grand Canary? In the dense mist that so often shrouds this group we could not tell. Moreover, our dead reckoning said one thing and our observations another. They usually do.

"When in doubt, heave to," was a maxim of the Skipper's that we happened to remember, so we hove to and waited, though for what I am not quite clear. If it were for the mist to disperse, I am inclined to think we should be there still. Steve and I passed the time in heated discussions as to our whereabouts, which under the circumstances was as futile an occupation as any we could have indulged in, but what would you? After golf it is doubtful if there is anything more debatable than incipient navigation. We continued to talk, and the dream ship continued to rock idly on a heavy swell, until Peter broke the spell by emitting a well-known squeak of excitement and pointing heavenward.

"*That* isn't a cloud," she announced with apparent irrelevance.

It was not. It was the peak of Teneriffe towering out of the mist, to port, like the great pyramid from the sands of Egypt.

"There you are," quoth Steve.

"Exactly," said I, though what either of us meant I have no notion.

"In the meantime," suggested Peter the practical, "don't you think we might be getting on with it?"

On this point the master and the mate of the dream ship were agreed, and the voyage continued.

THE START ACROSS THE ATLANTIC

Visitations—pleasant, and the reverse

CHAPTER V

Visitations—pleasant, and the reverse

Our entry into Las Palmas savoured of a circus come to town. We were the "act" where the music stops for effect. No one seemed to know who we were or why we were, which after all is not surprising, and the curious, consisting of gaping crowds on the breakwater and a heterogeneous fleet of anything from powerful launches to frowsy bumboats, seemed intent on finding out.

There is an immense and almost constant swell off Las Palmas, and the performance started when, in answer to our signal, a pilot stepped aboard, and came as near to measuring his dignified and bedizened length on the deck as was possible without actually doing it. He was evidently unused to dream ships in a swell. Regaining a certain amount of equilibrium, he tottered to the mast and clung there affectionately, until informed that we were from England, when he risked changing his grip to shake us all warmly by the hand, and point dramatically harbourward.

This last I took as a signal for the engine which, to my relief, "went," and we rounded the breakwater with the entire fleet of bumboats and their yelling occupants in our wake. Peter was at the tiller, in pyjamas she had not had time to change, frenziedly following the course indicated by the pilot's outstretched arm. Steve was attempting in halting Spanish to communicate the fact that our engine had no "reverse," and failing utterly. And I had made the distressing discovery that there was something amiss with our water circulation. Above all rose the clamour of the bum-boatmen:—"Hi, washing, Señor!" "Hi, hi, bananas!" "Hi, hi, hi...."

So the dream ship threaded the intricacies of Las Palmas's inner harbour, missing coal hulks by a bare foot, shaving schooners and, by means of the anchor dropped in sheer desperation, barely saving herself from ramming the Club Náutico.

Even then our troubles were by no means at an end. A boarding party of eternal bumboatmen broke through our defenses, and thronged the deck. In vain we pointed out that all we needed at the moment was sleep, and that if they had any for sale we would buy large quantities, otherwise they must go, or be pushed. They chose to be pushed, and there was something in the nature of a *mêlée* afoot when a sleek launch came alongside and a short, corpulent gentleman, literally glittering with gold lace, and using a sword as a walking stick, stepped aboard. He was the chief of the harbour police, and the effect of his august presence was magical. The enemy retired in disorder, and our saviour, who honoured us with his company over a glass of rum, gave us the key to peace and quiet in a Spanish port. It consisted in presenting the law (embodied in himself) with a trifling donation, and running the international code flag "P" up to the mast head, after which one is at liberty to shoot any one who comes aboard without permission. It is worth knowing, for we of the dream ship did both these things, and from that hour suffered no further molestation.

Unless you are a coal magnate, a ship's chandler, a banana agent, or a consumptive, it is hard to find a reason for living at Las Palmas. It is a dreary sort of place built on, and occasionally smothered by, sand blown across the ocean from the Sahara, hundreds of miles distant, and the only diversion appears to be dances and roulette at the Club Náutico.

We of the dream ship promptly "fell" for the roulette, in company with most of the inhabitants, until it was borne in upon us that if we "fell" much further we should plumb the depths of our slender resources. It is a pathetic sight to see workers, not the leisured "profitocracy" one encounters at a place like Monte Carlo, handing over their hard-earned week's wage to a stony-faced *croupier*, and borrowing from any one who will lend for "just one more spin." No, we remained for the most part well out amongst the cooler breezes of the harbour, under the thrice-blessed squaresail which now did service as an awning—sleeping, swimming, fishing, and again sleeping, for we had some arrears to make up in this last respect.

Our splendid isolation, however, did not prevent us from meeting interesting people, foremost amongst whom was the skipper of the four-masted schooner *Dorothy* of New York, a hard-bitten Yank if ever there was one. He caught us clinging to his anchor chain for a breather during the morning swim, and was treating us to an entirely new vocabulary of invective when suddenly, and with no apparent cause, he changed his mind and invited us aboard.

In his remarkably comfortable quarters, and standing in pools of our own making, we discussed things in general and a bottle of Madeira in particular.

"Waal," he observed, on learning that we were off "that funny bit of wood yonder," and had every intention of remaining on it across the Atlantic, "if you ain't got a gall!"

Swimmers at Dorothy

From that moment the *Dorothy* and the dream ship became "matey craft," though a greater contrast than between a four-masted schooner and a twenty-three-ton cutter can scarcely be imagined. Our friend had several grievances, and aired them, though with such cheerful profanity as to cause us endless amusement. He had left the sea for good when he was lured out of retirement by a stupendous sum to command the *Dorothy*. The fact was they had no sailing masters in the States these days, and now that they had found wind to be cheaper than coal, and were building schooners so fast that half of them were green timber and opened up like sieves, they could get no one to take charge—no one, that is, but hairless boys who learnt navigation on a three-weeks' course, and knew as much about seamanship or handling the hoboes one ships these days as a dead-ripe lemon....

At this juncture Steve and I might have been seen to exchange guilty glances, but I don't think we were, and the diatribe continued.

... Another thing: here was he at a port like Las Palmas, with his entire crew, bar the mate, in a Spanish gaol through a few shore indiscretions of the previous evening, and no one to *do* anything about it. There was no United

States consul in Las Palmas, no, sir; what did we think of that? There was nothing against a bit of shore joy once in a while. It was to be expected. But when they took a man's *cook*.... He would have to see his very good friend the British Consul about it, that was all, though the idea was abhorrent to his independent spirit.

Amongst other things he treated us to a vivid and somewhat terrifying picture of present-day New York, and expressed the whole-souled wish never to return. It appeared that in this barbarous spot a mere man is at a discount. He can get nothing to drink. His pipe, cigar, or cigarette is in imminent peril of being snatched from his mouth, and if he chances to look sideways at a lady she arrests him on the spot. We shivered in unison, and refilled our glasses.

Our friend dined aboard the dream ship that evening, and showed himself to be the good fellow that he was by demonstrating short cuts in navigation, telling us of winds and weather we should be likely to encounter, giving us introductions to friends at distant ports, and—listening without flinching to a clarionet solo. It is such members of the vast fraternity of the sea that one hopes to meet again, and so rarely does.

Another of our guests was of a very different calibre, though none the less interesting in his way. We awoke one morning to find a sleek white yacht of about the dream ship's tonnage anchored hard by, and flying a silken flag of gorgeous but unknown design, which on book reference proved to be the now-extinct emblem of the Portuguese Royalist.

By noon her owner had paid us a formal call, and at four o'clock this amazing youth, in a natty naval uniform garnished with decorations for various heroic deeds, was laying bare his heart in excellent English over a cup of afternoon tea. It was good, he informed us, to see the Blue Ensign again after what he had been through. There was something stable about the Blue Ensign that was vastly refreshing to a homeless exile. During the present welter of world upheaval the Portuguese rebellions had been overlooked, but what he, a Royalist, had been through—*what* he had been through!

His was the only yacht in Portuguese waters during the late rebellion. She lay in the bay of Funchal, Madeira, and in Madeira's gaol reposed, or at any rate contrived to live, two full-blown counts, a general, and various smaller fry, incarcerated for their political views. Could a fellow Royalist and a yacht owner stand by and do nothing under such circumstances? A thousand times, no! On a dark night, and in face of sentries armed to the teeth, he had rescued them, taken them aboard his ship, and set sail for Las Palmas without stores, water, or navigation instruments, fearing that any such preparations would arouse suspicion. Well, he had arrived. After incredible hardships, he had arrived, only to have his yacht and cargo of hungry counts interned by the rascally Spaniard! Another cup of tea? Ah, thanks ... to the CAUSE!

The Portuguese says: "A Spaniard is always a Spaniard." The Spaniard says: "A Portuguese is always a Portuguese." Or they do at Las Palmas, and the mere outsider can only take their respective words for it, and draw his own conclusions.

After two weeks of idling—and cooking—we became so heartily tired of the latter that we determined to indulge in the wild extravagance of a cook. The process of engagement was simplicity itself. We merely selected one of the almost constant stream of applicants for work that visited the dream ship, duly installed him in the fo'c's'le, and left him to it.

Our selection, or rather Peter's, as we left such things to a woman's alleged intuition, was a venerable Maltese with a sheaf of credentials the size of a pack of cards, and a winning if somewhat weak smile. Thereafter, for a week, real food, though doused in olive oil, emerged from the fo'c's'le, and we experienced the keen satisfaction after meals of being able to hold a cigarette in one hand without a dish cloth in the other.

This happy state of affairs continued until, following one of his "evenings off," our cook was stricken with an illness that he ascribed to bad meat, though the symptoms corresponded more to the effects of bad drink. In any case, he lay writhing in his bunk, clasping various portions of his anatomy, and declaring that he was about to die. Now, the dream ship had a medicine chest of which she was as proud as the eminent physician who had selected it. This personage believed in injection rather than internal application; and no doubt he was right, provided there was someone aboard who understood a hypodermic syringe. But there was not. I stood beside the bunk, looking up the unhappy man's symptoms in a ship's medical guide as they occurred, while Steve and Peter lifted from its bed of cotton wool a glass-and-steel instrument more like an overgrown mosquito than anything I can call to mind. The look of it appalled me, but not so Steve. He pumped our wretched cook so full of laudanum that he never moved an eyelid for fifteen hours. We called his state one of merciful oblivion, and rather prided ourselves on the achievement until it occurred to someone that we might have killed him. Followed frantic tests with a looking-glass, and much listening for heart-beats, until our victim was resuscitated—and left the next day.

No, in future, and in spite of expert advice to the contrary, which perhaps does not take the limitations of dream ships into account, I shall in future only take the trusted remedies endeared by experience: iodine, a good aperient and astringent, asperin, plenty of boracic lint and bandages, and a lancet.

As though in judgment, there descended upon us in turn a plague of these islands called Canary fever. It was our first and last illness throughout the cruise, but it pulled us down to such an extent that Peter and I decided to try the hills of Grand Canary as a recuperative.

A quiet little *fonda* amongst the vines and purer airs of the highlands was the vision that lured us into a lurching motor, and up through the sand and cactus landscape to Fergus, where our vision was shattered as promptly and effectually as visions usually are. There was a *fonda*, and there were cacti, these last covered for the most part with the cochineal beetle, the raising of which as a food dyestuff is still an industry on Grand Canary, though chemical substitutes have almost run the genuine article off the market. But the *fonda* was more crowded with guests than the cacti with cochineal, and there was no doubt as to which were the more disturbing.

Peter and I shared a room nine by twelve, with an apology for privacy in the form of a riddled screen between us, and mosquitoes took full advantage of our netless beds. The *salon* at our very door seethed with dancing and shrill-voiced señoritas until two o'clock in the morning, and—— But why prolong the agony? We caught the next lurching motor back to Las Palmas, and sank gasping but grateful into deck chairs under the awning of the dream ship.

Such a home as ours spoils one for roughing it. The infinite peace and quiet and privacy of it make one detest all the more the bustle and turmoil of ordinary travel. People have said to me: "But how can you live in such restricted quarters?" My answer is: "Very easily, thank you."

For six mortal weeks we waited at Las Palmas, that it might be fulfilled which was spoken by the weather-prophets concerning the West Indian hurricane season:

June, too soon.

July, stand by.

August, if you must.

September, remember.

October, all over.

And on the third of this last, reassuring month we set sail across the Atlantic.

THE ARRIVAL AT BRITISH WEST INDIES

*Deep-sea thoughts—Concerning Calms—Visitors in
mid-Atlantic—Barbados and beyond*

CHAPTER VI

*Deep-sea thoughts—Concerning Calms—Visitors in
mid-Atlantic—Barbados and beyond*

The great adventure had now begun in earnest. Three thousand miles of
Atlantic Ocean lay ahead of us, holding we knew not what of new experience,
and for the third time since setting sail our undertaking imbued us with a
certain amount of awe.

At night, alone in the cockpit, one began to think. Would the drinking water
hold out? What if the chronometer broke down? Supposing—— It is as well
not to think too deeply on occasion, and the crossing of the Atlantic in a
small boat is one.

Someone has said that it is the routine of life that keeps us sane, and I am
inclined to agree. On shore, one is apt to inveigh against "the little things that
must be done"—the countless, almost mechanical actions of a day's civilized
existence—but at sea life is composed of such details, and one is thankful for
them. Making a long-splice or an "eye," filling and trimming the lamps,
washing down deck, or even washing up dishes, all serve to keep the mind
from unhealthy conjecture.

Sleep was again our worst enemy at the tiller. Staring into the lighted binnacle
with its swaying compass card, or down at the phosphorescent water swirling
and hissing past the ship's stern, the helmsman became as one hypnotized.
It seemed that he was not of this world, but an atom hurtling through space.
The temptation was to surrender himself to the sensuous joy of it, a
temptation resisted only by an almost painful effort, and the knowledge that
the lives of all aboard depend on his keeping his leaden eyelids from closing
down.

A four-hour watch as helmsman is too long. They do not allow it in the
mercantile marine; but what were we to do? Steve confessed to recalling all
the poetry that he knew, consisting of most of Kipling, the whole of Omar
Khayyam, and sundry doubtful limericks; then attempting to say them
backward. Peter hummed over her repertoire of songs, or thought out new
dishes for her week's cookment. As for me, I kept a marlinspike handy, and
when oblivion threatened used it.

It will be seen that a dream ship is not all dream. If it were, such is the
perversity of human nature, the dreamer would probably be tired of it within
a month.

"I can promise you the northeast 'trades' the whole way across," said our
friend of the five-masted schooner at Las Palmas, turning the pages of his
log. Also, the wind chart sported a reassuring number of long-shafted arrows

pointing from that quarter for the month of October. These things may account for the fact that not one day's northeast wind did we encounter on the Atlantic passage. It seems that the elements have a rooted objection to being anticipated. We could have crossed in an open boat for all of the weather, and three becalmed days in mid-ocean we occupied in swimming round the ship, or diving to scrape the barnacles off her copper.

But stark calms are a wearisome business. Every function of a ship has ceased. It is as though she lay dead in a stagnant pool, and any movement of spars or canvas were the rattling of her bones. Also, it is an aggravation to the restless insect called man, adrift in a breathless waste of waters, to know that leagues lie ahead of which he is incapable of covering a yard.

An auxiliary engine is useless under such circumstances. To use it is like hurrying on to catch a tram that is bound to overtake one in the long run. What is a steaming radius of four hundred miles in a stretch of three thousand? No, all one can do after satisfying himself that his vessel is "as idle as a painted ship upon a painted sea," is to pass the time as pleasantly as may be. We of the dream ship turned in and slept, or broke the uncanny silence with fearsome noises on clarionet and piano. Also, we fished, though with a lack of success that leads me to believe that fish do not bite in mid-ocean. At night flying fish struck the mainsail, and fell to the deck with a resounding thwack and a flutter of "wings," but for the most part on occasions when we had failed to hang a lantern in the rigging to attract them, which, as far as I am concerned, explodes another fallacy.

As day succeeded day, and there was no sign of a change in our inert condition, our thoughts turned again in the direction of the drinking water. True, we had two hundred gallons aboard, but what was to prevent us from being becalmed for a month, or being carried hundreds of miles out of our course by a gale, according to the mood of the capricious elements? We cut our daily allowance from a gallon to half a gallon per head for all purposes and, as though in response to our frugality, a breath came out of the southeast.

At the moment of its arrival Steve and I happened to be testing our sense of direction by diving overboard, and trying to come up through a lifebelt floating about ten yards distant. Steve had just conceived the brilliant idea of moving the belt after the diver had taken the plunge, and I had emerged from a lung-racking effort to locate it, when we realized that the dream ship had moved, in fact was still moving, with a noticeable wake in the direction of the horizon. The tiller was pegged amidships, and there was nothing to stop her continuing the motion indefinitely—except Peter, who was below. We prayed in that hour that she was not asleep.

Swimming near boat

I have often left home—perhaps too often—but this was the first occasion on which home looked as if it were leaving *me*, and in mid-Atlantic at that. Alternately we yelled and swam, but without gaining a foot until to our infinite relief a small, pyjamaed figure appeared on deck, threw up its arms in horror, and brought the dream ship into the wind.

An hour later we were bowling along at seven knots, revelling in the blessed motion of air, and planning what we should do when we reached Barbados, a mere fifteen hundred miles distant.

It was in mid-Atlantic, too, that we received visitors. The first were Mr. and Mrs. Smith, a devoted couple of fish about the size of a sprat, each decorated similarly with vivid green bands on an electric blue background. For four days they remained with us, swimming closely side by side under our idle propeller, presumably for shade. To lie on deck looking down into the limitless blue depths and watching our companions became the king of pastimes aboard the dream ship. We even tried to catch them with a minute hook and the tastiest of baits, but they would suffer no nearer acquaintance. They were too busy getting somewhere for some reason to swerve an iota from their course. During a squall we lost them, or they lost us; in any case, we never saw them again, and I have often wondered since what Mr. and Mrs. Smith are doing now.

The next guest was a black bird about the size of a crow, with webbed feet, a wicked-looking beak, and white circles round the eyes. He was a sick and sorry bird when he fluttered on to the rudder top during a rain squall, edged slowly along the tiller, and over Peter's hand into her lap, where she covered him with her oilskin and he lay content. But his was a flying visit in more than one sense of the word, for he refused to eat. Bread crumbs, morsels of flying fish, and meat were offered him, but he spurned them all, and grew so weak that when carried into the scuppers by the ship's lurching two days later, he rose in the air and was carried off into the turmoil of wind and wave. The last we saw of him was a bunch of black feathers on the face of a comber, still struggling to rise.

What with weather ranging all the way from stark calms to vicious squalls, and a correspondingly varied progress of anything from ten to two hundred miles in the twenty-four hours, it took us thirty days to cross the Atlantic, and when it was done we spent the best part of a day trying to find the proof of our accomplishment in the island of Barbados. Faulty navigation again? Yes, but it is not the easiest thing in life to make a "bow on" landfall of a clod of earth twenty-one miles by twelve after a three-thousand-mile jaunt to reach it. Also, we suspected our chronometer.

When Barbados, after the fashion of Grand Canary, failed to materialize, we of the dream ship held one of our now familiar board meetings. There were two courses open: to emulate the mariner of old who knew nothing of longitude, and cruise along our latitude until Barbados appeared; or to head for Trinidad instead, and so have the coastline of South America as a buffer if we failed to make it.

We had decided on the latter course, and were actually standing away for Trinidad, when Barbados, a mere wraith of land that we scarce dared to believe in, beckoned us from the southern horizon. We accepted the invitation.

The first human face other than our own that we had seen for a solid month was that of the "outside man" of Messrs. —— & Co., and as a change we welcomed it. He came to us in a natty whaleboat propelled by a crew of hefty Negro oarsmen, showed us the best anchorage, and saw us safely berthed before allowing the fact to emerge that he was an "outside man," that his particular firm could do anything for a ship cheaper, quicker, and better than any in Bridgetown, and that our patronage was the one thing he had been craving ever since our approach had been made known from the signal station. I shall be surprised on my next visit to Barbados, which I hope will not be long delayed, if that "outside man" is not a director of Messrs. —— & Co.

I may add that our first care was to take our erring chronometer to be readjusted, and the mainspring broke the next day. That is how near we had been to disaster in the Atlantic.

While a new mainspring was being fitted and rated, we gladly surrendered ourselves to the tender mercies of the most charming, hospitable people one could wish to meet. My recollections of our two-weeks' sojourn are a trifle vague owing to the rapidity with which one pleasure succeeded another. I remember lying at anchor with awnings up in the most beautiful bay it is possible to imagine, and sleeping twenty-four hours on end. From then onward life consisted of "swizzles," car rides over a fairy-island, and more swizzles, pony races to the accompaniment of swizzles, surf bathing followed by swizzles, and evenings at the Savannah Club, where conversation was punctuated and sometimes drowned by the concoction of yet more swizzles by a hard-worked army of coloured folk behind a gleaming mahogany bar.

There is no escaping the "swizzle" in Barbados—even if one wished to, which personally I did not. It is a delightful, healthful drink composed of the very best rum, angostura bitters, syrup, fresh lime, nutmeg, and ice—the whole "swizzled" to the creamy consistency of—— But I forget that I may be addressing a country in the grip of total abstinence, and whatever my faults I have never been accused of making a man's mouth water without supplying the deficiency.

Before the war the Barbados estate owner was on the verge of bankruptcy. Now he is probably the most prosperous landed proprietor in the world. It matters not whether he be white or black, or any one of the intermediary shades, he is keeping up a luxurious establishment, driving his car in a cloud of dust and dignity from one end of the island to the other, or installing a manager (usually some hopeless wight who was absent on duty during the war) and taking up residence in Park Lane or Fifth Avenue according to taste. And "sugar" is the answer. Sugar is king of Barbados, and it were easier for the proverbial camel to pass through the needle's eye than for the outsider to buy, beg, borrow, or steal a square foot of his domain.

It is difficult to see just what will happen to Barbados in the future unless some outlet is found for the Negro population. Already this minute island is the second most densely populated spot in the world—the first being a certain district of China—and there seems no other alternative than for it to populate itself into the sea. The United States is imposing drastic restrictions on Negro immigration, as evidenced by the surging and expectant, though mostly disappointed, crowds that assemble outside the American Consulate in Bridgetown daily. The self-governing British Dominions will have none of them. Where are they to go? Meantime, they grow—Lord, how they grow!—in numbers and insolence.

Hot foot from a ball at one of the hotels, we literally fled aboard ship and sailed by stealth; otherwise I am convinced that we should be at Barbados tennising, surfing, dancing, pony racing, and "swizzling" to this day.

Even then we weighed anchor one evening only to drop it the next off Soutrier, a town on the fairy island of St. Lucia where we had been invited to stay on a plantation. Our host, as kindly a soul as ever lived, insisted that it would do us all a power of good to leave the dream ship in charge of one of his boys—or a dozen of them if we preferred—and have a real rest and change at his house. And a rest and change it undoubtedly was. From doing everything for ourselves, our régime changed abruptly to one of being prevented by an army of well-trained house-boys from so much as turning a hand.

The West Indian planter is a man to be envied. He lives in one of the beauty spots of the world, and neither the servant problem nor "high cost of living" affects him to anything like the same extent as others. This home that we of the dream ship had invaded was a miracle of cool, well-ordered comfort, set high on the wooded hillside, commanding by day an endless vista of palm-clad mountain and sparkling Caribbean, and by night encompassed with perfumed darkness, the glint of fireflies, and the vocal efforts of the whistling frog—a nimble little fellow, green as an emerald and no larger than a pea.

The plantation, which only five years previously had been virgin jungle, was devoted to limes and cocoa, both of which grow to perfection in the West Indies, and as a commercial enterprise threaten in time to dethrone King Sugar. Here on St. Lucia, as elsewhere in the West Indies, there is unlimited scope for the smaller man who stands no chance on Barbados and the more thickly settled islands. Indeed, after having spent most of my life roaming about the world, I can never understand why a man with strictly limited capital will buy or lease land, however cheap, in the furthermost corners of the earth, thousands of costly miles from his market, and where he will most certainly have to pay anything from a dollar to five dollars a day for indifferent labour, while in the West Indies there is still land to be had as rich as any in the world, plantation labour—and good labour at that—is a shilling per day per head, and New York is five, and London ten days distant. I can only attribute it to the lure of "green fields that are ever far off."

THROUGH THE PANAMA CANAL

From Atlantic to Pacific, and the strange happenings
that intervened

CHAPTER VII

From Atlantic to Pacific, and the strange happenings
that intervened

"Look out for the Caribbean Sea toward December," was another axiom of our five-masted-schooner friend at Las Palmas, but he proved no less fallible over the passage from Barbados to Colon than he had concerning the Atlantic. In fact, I am thinking of in future asking advice of weather prophets in order to anticipate the reverse.

A spanking wind on the quarter, with mainsail and squaresail set, and a mighty following sea that flung the dream ship before it in a series of exhilarating swoops, brought us within sight of land in seven days, a distance of twelve hundred miles. But what land? For a time we were at a loss. Comparing it with the chart and descriptions in "sailing directions" revealed nothing. It was a low-lying, mist-enshrouded, sinister-looking land, and we sailed along its coast for a day and a night before we could tell whether we had passed Colon or hit the coast to the eastward.

Ultimately, a lighthouse gave us the clue, and we found that owing to a current that has the unpleasant knack of running at anything from a half to three knots we were still fifty miles from our objective, so we headed for sea and hove to until daylight.

All night as we lay rolling in a heavy swell steamers passed us by, floating palaces of light, and with the dawn we joined the procession of giants making for the Panama Canal.

We wished to go through the canal? Very well; a measurer would be sent off to decide our tonnage, and we must be ready to take the pilot aboard at five o'clock the next morning.

That, in effect, is what the canal authorities said, and I answered it with a smile that I trust was sufficiently engaging to hide the fact that I was not at all sure we had enough money between us to pay the tolls. It must be an expensive business, this passing from Atlantic to Pacific. I had never thought of that. There was quite a lot I had not thought about. What if the charges were altogether beyond us? It would mean Cape Horn! Cape Horn or the abandonment of the dream! Which was worse for one who, after sixty below zero on the Canadian prairie, four below zero in France and Belgium, and something far worse in coalless London, had taken a solemn oath never again to leave the forties of latitude!

These terrifying reflections were cut short by a voice.

"I can't make it more than twelve tons."

"Twelve tons?"

The canal official deigned to exhibit surprise by a slight elevation of the eyebrows, then smiled.

"The measurer has been aboard," he told me, "and you are twelve tons net. The tolls will be fifteen dollars. Will you pay now, or at the other end?"

Such was my relief that I paid on the spot, thereby reducing our united capital to £20—or, at the then-prevailing rate of exchange, seventy-eight dollars.

This brief interview with officialdom is typical of Panama Canal methods. Speed, silence, efficiency; nothing else "goes" in "the Zone." Things are done in a few seconds and utter silence here that would take hours and pandemonium elsewhere. The entire miracle of passing a ten-thousand-ton liner from Atlantic to Pacific through seven locks and forty miles of tortuous, ever-threatening channels has been performed in six and a half hours, and with a lack of fuss that is almost uncanny.

But the dream ship was twelve tons, and not ten thousand, and for that reason it is probable that she gave more trouble than any craft since the canal was opened. Yet on every hand we received the utmost courtesy and kindness. Such treatment made us feel like pestiferous mosquitoes being politely conducted to the door instead of squashed flat on the spot as we deserved. But you shall see.

Punctually at five A.M., the pilot came aboard in his immaculate white drill uniform and, without a smile at his surroundings, including ourselves in variegated costume, took up his position in the bows. I went below, and after a ten-minutes' wrestle with the auxiliary, contrived to make three out of the four cylinders "go" sufficiently to propel us at the dignified speed of three knots in the direction of the canal.

"Is that the best she can do?" enquired the pilot.

I lifted an apologetic, perspiring, and begrimed face to him and admitted that it was. Moreover, that we were very lucky to be doing that.

"Ah, well, the day is young," he commented, cheerfully. "What about an awning? We shall be baked alive before we've done."

Did I tell him that the reason we had not rigged an awning was that I was more than half expecting the engine to break down, and that we should have to hoist sail? I did not. Whoever heard of sailing through the Panama Canal? An awning was rigged, and we entered Gatun Lock in style, followed by two more liners.

The giant gates closed. There was an eruption of water seemingly under our stern that caused the tiller to fly over and extract a groan of anguish from

Steve as it crushed him against the cock-pit wall; the aft warp snapped, and the dream ship commenced to rise, more like an elevator than a ship in a lock, until the blank, greasy wall ended, and above it appeared a row of grinning faces.

"That's that," said the pilot; and it was.

By some miracle the engine carried us to the next lock, where the same performance was gone through, with such slight variations as the loss of a hat, three fenders, and the remainder of the port covering-board.

We passed out into Gatun Lake, a fairy place of verdure-clad islets and mist-enshrouded reaches, where cranes flew low over the water, and strange, wild cries came out of the bush.

It was also the place where our engine refused its office peremptorily, irrevocably. I was engineer of the dream ship, probably the worst on earth, but still, the engineer, and for an agonized hour I wrestled with lifeless scrap-iron. How the profession of marine motor engineering ever attracts adherents it is beyond me to imagine. I know one man it has sent to an asylum, and many others who to this day bear the marks of having trifled with it—finger-nails that nothing short of cutting to the quick and gouging with a shovel will render clean; hands, clothes, and for some unknown reason face ingrained with ineradicable grime; a permanently furrowed brow; and a wistful expression that goes to the heart of the beholder.

Egret, crocodile

In order to avoid such a fate I have made it a practice to try hard for one solid hour and, failing to gain a response from the atrocity, leave the matter in other, and perhaps more capable, hands. I communicated this information to the pilot, and there and then the man's more human side came to the surface. It was raining as it knows how to rain on the Isthmus, he was soaked to the hide, his natty uniform resembled nothing more closely than a dish rag, yet he smiled, and proceeded to remove his jacket.

"Guess we'd better sail," he said.

Behold once more the dream ship sailing through the Panama Canal; alternately scudding before rain squalls, lying becalmed, and making tacks of fifty yards and less, a passage surely unique in the annals of "the Zone." The pilot said he enjoyed it, and by the way he swigged on halyards and gave us an old-time chanty to work by, I am inclined to believe him. We were lucky in our pilot.

Toward evening, and during a stark calm, Steve dived overboard and made us fast to a light-buoy, his jaw dropping perhaps half an inch, and a thoughtful expression coming into his eyes, when a little later a log on the muddy shore was suddenly imbued with life, and slipped into the water with a whisk of a horny tail.

So it was that we had afternoon tea in comfort, some alleged music on piano and clarionet, and a pleasant chat with the pilot concerning the older and better days of the wind-jammer, while dainty egrettes watched us from a tree fern, ungainly pelicans swooped and dived, and somewhere ten-thousand-ton liners were being hustled through the Panama Canal.

We had no wireless, that was why it was impossible to summon a tug to take us on our way, but finally a monstrous steamer passed so close that it was possible to hail her, and a few hours later we were taken in tow by an apparition of noiseless engines, shining varnish, and gleaming brass.

It would cost us six dollars an hour, the pilot told us, and I sat back to figure out just how long seventy-eight dollars would last under such an onslaught. The result was alarming. We held a board meeting about it in the bows, and decided there was nothing for it but to go on, and keep going on, until we stopped. We had hoped to reach lands where money was of secondary importance, but we were not there yet, that was evident.

So we continued to race through the canal at the rate of six dollars an hour until we reached the approaches to Pedro Miguel lock, where the apparition tied us up and steamed off, still at six dollars an hour.

Something happened to us that night at Pedro Miguel. Looking back on it all I can hardly persuade myself that it was not a dream. We met some canal officials, tall, sun-burned youths with the mark of efficiency upon them yet with a merry twinkle in the eye. We asked them aboard, and they came and marvelled at what they saw. Their verdict was, as far as I remember: "Some novelty!" Then they asked us ashore, and it was our turn to marvel. One of our hosts was the chief operator of a lock, and we saw the miracle of the Isthmus of Panama from behind. Futility overwhelms me at the thought of trying to describe what we saw that night, over the lock, under the lock, at the sides of the lock; besides, you will find it all reduced to cold figures in technical journals if you are that way inclined. It was the spirit of the thing that took hold of me: a pigmy man sitting at a lever! What was not possible after this?

We returned to the ship almost stupefied. One feels much the same when he attempts to think in Westminster Abbey. We were in the process of turning in when a cheerful head appeared through the skylight.

"We await your pleasure," quoth a voice.

I explained that the owner of the head was no doubt unconsciously violating, but still violating, the sanctity of my sister's bedroom. It made no difference. I protested that at that moment my sister's costume consisted of a pair of ill-fitting pyjamas and a kimono; that Steve and I had nothing to our backs but what we had worn all day—an undershirt and a pair of football shorts; that we were all tired to death and literally ached for our pillows; that his kindness was overwhelming but that—— Nothing made any difference.

Somehow we found ourselves in a car, the chief operator's first car that he had learnt to drive during the dinner hour the previous day. Out into the moonlight we sped, or rather zigzagged, at the rate of forty, while between Peter and myself a youth named Bill—I shall never forget Bill—kept up a running flow of informative rhetoric: "*On* the left we have the famous Isthmus of Panama, intersected by the still more famous canal, a miracle of modern engineering, as it has been aptly termed. Fear not, lady!" [this in an aside to Peter] "the man at the wheel values his life as much as yours, perhaps more. *And now* we approach the historic city of Panama, passing on our left the Union Club, otherwise known as the Onion Club, frequented solely by the nobility and gentry of the neighbourhood, hence our exclusion. *And on the right*——"

On the right was the blazing portico of a cabaret, and the car had come to a jarring full stop.

In vain we pleaded our costume, the hour of night the utter degradation of exposing ourselves to the public gaze in such a condition. We literally found ourselves at a table drinking imitation lager beer and grape juice, and listening to raucous-voiced imported ladies rendering washy ballads to the accompaniment of tinkling ice and tobacco smoke.

It all sounds sordid enough, but it was vastly amusing to sea-weary wanderers, and will remain with us a memory of kindness and good-fellowship.

So, at last, we lay at anchor off Balboa on the Pacific Ocean. We had come far adown the vista of our dream, and hoped to go a great deal farther. To do so, we came to the conclusion that it would be necessary to make some money. How? Well, we had a dream ship, a group of pearling islands lay thirty miles to the eastward, and——

A strange life, my masters, but one that I would not exchange with any man on earth.

THE GALAPAGOS ISLANDS

The ash heap

CHAPTER VIII

The ash heap

When Balboa came to Balboa, it is safe to say that no ice cream awaited him there. Indeed, according to history the place was little more than a mosquito-infested swamp, and that is where we of the dream ship had the pull over Señor Balboa.

The town is in the Canal Zone, which is United States territory, though cutting clean through the Republic of Panama, and in this particular sample of United States territory, though founded upon a swamp, you will encounter—among other such amazing things as an entire absence of mosquitoes, charming residences set in park-like surroundings, and a well-conducted club free to all—an assortment of ice-cream creations warranted to hypnotize the uninitiated.

I have to mention this seemingly trivial detail because our lives at Balboa appeared to consist in rowing ashore to transact important business in Panama, and being waylaid en route and held captive by insidious messes.

Besides, it was over a Something Sundae that I met the man who came very near to shaping our destiny. True, there were pearling islands to the eastward, he informed me; he had fished there himself in the past with varying success, and would like nothing better than to try again aboard the dream ship. He would make enquiries.

The fruits of these were imparted the next day over a Peach Something Else. The group had been done to death, and was "closed" for a term of three years, but—this over an Orange Orangoutang—if we cared to go a little farther afield, and divert our attention from pearl shell to gold, he knew of a spot not far south where the natives were in the habit of washing the stuff out of clods of earth from their backyards, held under the eaves of the houses during a rain storm. What about it? The answer at the moment, and as far as I can remember, was a Strawberry Slush.

But we had decided to go. Preparations for making the wherewithal we so sorely needed were already afoot when a miracle intervened. On succeeding one afternoon in getting clean past temptation and into the city of Panama, I found a letter awaiting me from a certain magician who dwells in a place called New York. To hide the truth no longer, he had sold a story of mine to the "movies" at a figure that to our starved gaze looked like the war indemnity, and inside of a week the amount, in beautiful, round, twenty-dollar gold pieces, littered the cabin table of the dream ship.

I am aware that in most accounts of travel such sordid details as the financial difficulties encountered are invariably omitted, either because there were none, or because the writer considers it in the light of bad form to mention them. In our particular case they certainly existed, and personally I am not very strong on form. After all, money is a means to an end—even to the realization of a dream, and I can only say that ours would have evaporated into thin air at Balboa but for the miracle performed by the magician in New York.

On the strength of our sudden affluence, the dream ship received a sleek and well-deserved coat of paint, a new main sheet of good manila, a hundred gallons of kerosene, a fresh supply of provisions, and incidentally a new lease of life.

She sailed in charge of a genial pilot who seemed as pleased as his confrère of the canal at being under sail again, and sighed wistfully on taking his leave at the last fairway buoy. There are many such men engaged in the routine of life, who long to break away and answer the call of the sea and adventure, but who rarely do, either because they cannot or have not the courage of their dream.

We had been advised that Panama Bay was a promising trolling ground, and for once report spoke true, for we caught a fine bonito within an hour of our departure. We were doing about five knots at the time, and it was a fine sight to see a fifteen-pound fish leaping and splashing astern; and a still finer to see sections of him sizzling in the frying pan.

A very different class of fish visited us a day or two later but, spurning our spoon bait, gave his attention to the log. A large shark, looking like a sinister shadow in the turmoil of our wake, investigated the twinkling fan with interest. Five times he approached it and withdrew, before risking indigestion and swallowing it whole.

As about a week later precisely the same thing occurred to our last remaining fan, from then onward we were bereft of log and "dead reckoning" at one fell swoop. However, as the sun is an almost constant companion in these latitudes, and the chronometer, after a thorough overhauling at Panama, appeared to be behaving itself, the loss was not as serious as might be expected.

Each day now brought us appreciably nearer the Equator, and its presence began to make itself felt in gasping moments at the tiller, a glare from the water that caused blood-shot eyes until Peter the practical produced a pair of smoked glasses, and deck seams running and bubbling marine glue.

Sailboat, shark

Peter's watch was a spectacle not to be missed, consisting as it did of pyjamas, smoked glasses, and a parasol! I have often wondered what sort of entertainment we should have provided for a passing steamer on occasion, but as we never sighted one from the beginning to the end of our cruise, I fear I shall never know.

"To-morrow," said Steve, after twelve days of fair though light winds, "we ought to raise Tower Island."

We were approaching the ash heap of the world. At the time we had no notion that it was an ash heap, but you shall judge. Throughout that night we took our appointed four-hour single-handed watch, slept our four hours as we had come mechanically so to do during the past four months, and went on deck at dawn to see Tower Island.

It was not there.

Steve, who was at the tiller, looked vaguely troubled, but offered no comment. Neither did we, by this time being used to such things. Besides, "Leave a man to his job," had become our watch-word through many vicissitudes. But when night followed day with customary inexorableness, and without producing anything more tangible than the same empty expanse of ocean, Steve was constrained to mutter, a sure preliminary to coherent speech.

"One of three things has happened," he announced: "the chronometer's got the jim-jams, the chart's wrong, or the blinking island has foundered."

As skipper of the dream ship, it devolved upon myself to verify these surprising statements, which, after a superhuman struggle, I did. By our respective observations and subsequent calculations the ship's position proved identical. According to instruments we were at that moment plumb in the middle of Tower Island. It was thoughtless of it to have evaporated at the very moment when we so sorely needed it as a landmark. We said so in strong terms. We were still saying something of the sort when a small, high-pitched voice came from aloft:

"Land O!"

Peter, in striped white-and-green pyjamas, was astride the jaws of the gaff. Steve and I exchanged relieved glances, and, with a lashed tiller, we all went below for a "swizzle," the now inevitable accompaniment to a landfall. We had reached the Galapagos Islands.

The southeast "trade" was blowing as steadily as a "trade" knows how, and there was nothing between us and Cristobal, the only inhabited island of the group; consequently, I slept the sleep of a mind at peace until awakened by a well-known pressure on the arm.

"Come and take a look at this," whispered Steve so as not to wake Peter in the opposite bunk.

"This" proved to be a solid wall of mist towering over the ship like a precipice. The trade wind had fallen to a stark calm, and the dream ship lay wallowing on an oily swell. A young moon rode clear overhead, and myriads of monstrous stars glared down at us; yet still this ominous gray wall lay fair in our path.

"It ought not to be land," said Steve, "but I don't like the look of it."

Neither did I. We stood side by side, straining our eyes into the murk. A soft barking, for all the world like that of a very old dog, sounded somewhere to port. Splashes, as of giant bodies striking the water, accompanied by flashes of phosphorescent light, came at intervals from all sides, and presently the faint lap of water reached our ears.

"Mother of Mike!" breathed Steve. "We're *alongside* something."

At that moment, and as though impelled by some silent mechanism, the pall of mist lifted, revealing an inky black wall of rock not fifty yards distant.

My frenzied efforts at the flywheel of the motor auxiliary were futile, as I had more than half expected. Who has ever heard of these atrocities answering in an emergency? We had no sweeps. To anchor was a physical impossibility; the lead-line vanished as probably twenty other lead-lines would have vanished after it in those fathomless waters. So we stood, watching the dream ship drift to her doom.

What happened during the next hour is as hard to describe as I have no doubt it will be to believe. The Galapagos Islands are threaded with uncertain currents, and one was setting us now on to the rocky face of an islet cut as clean and sheer to the sea as a slice of cheese. We should have touched but for our fending off. There is no other way of describing our antics than to say that we clawed our way along that rocky wall until at the end of it a faint air caught the jib, the foresail, the mainsail, and we stood away without so much as a scratch.

Sunrise that morning was the weirdest I have ever seen. There are over two thousand volcano cones in the Galapagos Islands, and apparently we were in the midst of them. On all hands and at all distances were rugged peaks one hundred to two thousand feet high, rising sheer from a rose-pink sea into a crimson sky. Sleek-headed seals broke water alongside, peered at us for a space with their fawnlike eyes, barked softly, and were gone. Pelicans soared above our truck, and fell like a stone on their prey. Tiny birds, yellow and red, flitted about the deck or flew through the skylights, and settled on the cabin fittings with the utmost unconcern. And down under, in the crystal-clear depths, vague shapes hovered constantly: sharks, dolphin, turtle, and ghastly devil fish.

All life seemed confined to water and air; never was dry land so desolate and sinister as those myriads of volcanic cones. Yet one of them was peopled with human beings. Which? We were lost, if ever a ship was lost, in the labyrinths of an ash heap.

All we knew was that Cristobal was the eastern-most of the group. We sailed east, only to be becalmed inside of an hour and to lose by current what we had gained by wind. Close to this same group a sailing vessel has been known to have her insurance paid before she reached port. The calms run in belts of varying widths, and unless a ship can be towed or kedged to one side or the other there is nothing to prevent her remaining in the same spot for six months. Our water would not last that time, and there is none on any of the islands except Cristobal. We began to think. We continued to think for four mortal days until the fitful southeast "trade" revived as by a miracle, and we were bowling along at a seven-knot clip. What a relief was the blessed motion of air! We hardly dared breathe lest it should drop.

It held, and we made what we took to be Cristobal. The dinghy was lowered, the ship cleaned up for port, and we began to discuss the possibilities of fresh milk, eggs, and bread. But it was not Cristobal Island. Neither were three others that we visited, all as alike as peas—a chain of ash heaps, an iron-bound coast of volcanic rock broken here and there by a dazzling coral beach.

I admit that to professional seafarers our inability to find Cristobal must appear ridiculous. For their benefit I would point out that we were not professional seafarers but a party of inconsequent and no doubt over-optimistic landlubbers engaged in the materialization of a dream—to cruise through the South Sea Islands in our own ship; that what navigation we knew had been learnt in three weeks; and that I would invite any one who fancies his bump of locality to test it in the Galapagos Islands.

We had more than half decided to cut out Cristobal and its five hundred inhabitants, and shape a course for the Society Islands, three thousand miles to the southwest'ard, when Steve gave a yell like a wounded pup.

"I see Dalrymple Rock," he chanted as one in a trance, with the binocular to his eyes. "I see Wreck Point, and a bay between 'em with houses on the beach. What more do you want?"

How supremely simple it was to recognize each feature by the chart—when there was an unmistakable landmark to go by. What fools we had been to—— But we left further recriminations till a later date. At the present moment it was necessary to enter Wreck Bay through a channel three hundred yards wide without a mark on either side in the teeth of a snorting "trade," and with a lee tide.

At one time during the series of short tacks that were necessary to get a "slant" for the anchorage we were not more than fifty yards from the giant emerald-green rollers breaking on Lido Point to port with the roar of thunder. To starboard one could see the fangs of the coral reef waiting for us to miss stays to rip the bottom out of us. But the dream ship did not miss stays, and finally we shot through the channel into Wreck Bay, and anchored in three fathoms off a rickety landing-stage.

While the agony of removing a three-weeks' beard was in progress a crowd had assembled on the beach, and presently a boatload of three put off to us. Steve, with his smattering of Spanish, received them at the companion with a new-born elegance that matched their own. They proved to be the owner of the island, a good-looking youth of about twenty-five; the chief of police (presumably "chief" because there is only one representative of the law in the

Galapagos), a swarthy Ecuadorean in a becoming poncho; and a little, wrinkled old man with a finely chiselled face and delicate hands.

The owner of Cristobal informed us in excellent French (he had been four years in Paris previous to marooning himself on his equatorial possession) that the island was ours, and the fulness thereof; that he also was ours to command, and would we dine with him that evening at the *hacienda*, it being New Year's eve?

The "chief" of police demanded our ship's papers, which, when placed in his hands, he gracefully returned without attempting to read, and gave his undivided attention to a rum "swizzle" and a cigar.

The little old man, whom we soon learnt to call "Dad," sat mum, with a dazed expression on his face and his head at an angle after the fashion of the deaf. When he spoke, which he presently did with an unexpectedness that was startling, it was in a low, cultured voice, and in English! "What about this Dutch war he had heard rumours of during the last year or two? With Germany, was it? Well, now, and who was winning? Over, eh?—and with the Allies on top? That was good, that was good!" He rubbed his wrinkled hands and glared round on the assembled company with an air of triumph, but without making any appreciable impression on the owner of Cristobal or the "chief" of police.

Dad was a type, if ever there was one, of the educated ne'er-do-well hidden away in the farthest corner of the earth to avoid those things which most of us deem so desirable. He had a split-bamboo house on the beach, a wife who could cook, freedom, and God's sunlight. What more did man desire? He had run away to sea at the age of seventeen, run away from sea two years later at the Galapagos Islands, and remained there ever since. This was the second time he had spoken English in fifty years, so we must excuse his halting diction, but the tales he could tell—the tales!

He was here when the pirates of the South American coast murdered for money, even as they have a knack of doing to this day, and hid the loot at their headquarters in the Galapagos Islands, silver and gold, boatloads of it. He had built a cutter with his own hands, and sailed in search of this same loot, only to encounter the sole owner, still guarding his ill-gotten gains though reduced to nakedness and hair. At a distance Dad had seen him first, and, mistaking him for a mountain goat, had shot him through the heart. It was the first man he had killed, and he could not stay on the island after that—especially at night.

Afterward, I asked the owner of Cristobal if one might believe half the old man said, and he nodded gravely.

"There is much, also, that he does not say," he added with a smile.

There is undoubtedly treasure still lying hidden in the Galapagos Islands. Two caches have been unearthed, silver ingots and pieces of eight respectively. The finder of one built himself a handsome hotel in Ecuador, and the other drank himself to death in short order. But there is definite proof that there is more.

As a field for the treasure hunter it is doubtful if any place in the world offers better chances of success to-day than the Galapagos Islands, but—and there is always a "but"—the uncertainty of wind and current amongst the islands makes it impossible for a sailing ship to undertake the search, a motor auxiliary is too unreliable, and a small steamer is too large for the creeks and reef channels it would be necessary to negotiate. With a full-powered launch and diving apparatus, and a parent ship in attendance, and unlimited time, and patience, and money—but these be dreams beyond the reach of the penniless world-wanderer: dreams, nevertheless, that will assuredly one day be realized.

No one thinks of the Galapagos Islands. Situated a bare six hundred miles from the American coastline in the direct trade route between the South Pacific Islands and the United States of America, this group is seldom visited more than twice a year, and then for the most part by Ecuadorean schooners. The veriest atoll in the South Pacific receives more attention, and with not a tithe of the cause. The cause? Well, come with us to the *hacienda* of the owner of Cristobal and you shall see.

For this purpose it is necessary to transfer one's activities from the heaving deck of the dream ship to the equally heaving back of a mountain pony, and lope for an hour up a winding, boulder-strewn track through a wilderness of low scrub and volcanic rock. "Still an ash heap," you think, "nothing but an ash heap."

Then you surmount a ridge, the last of half a dozen, and rein in to breathe your pony and incidentally to marvel. You remind yourself that you are precisely on the Equator; yet it is positively chilly up here. A green, gently undulating country, dotted with grazing cattle and horses, patches of sugar-cane, coffee bushes, and lime trees, stretches away to a cloud-capped range of mountains.

The soil is a rich red loam, almost stoneless, and scarcely touched with the plough. There are three thousand five hundred head of cattle at present on Cristobal Island, and it could support fifty thousand with ease. There is no disease and no adverse climatic condition with which to contend, and at three years old a steer brings one hundred dollars (gold), live weight, at Guayaquil—when a steamer can be induced to call and take it there.

There are a few hundred acres under cultivation when there ought to be thousands, and two hundred bone-lazy peons do the work of fifty ordinary farm hands.

Looking down on this fertile valley it is hard to realize that one is standing on the lip of a long-extinct crater, that in reality Cristobal is a series of these, dour and uninviting to a degree, viewed from outside, but veritable gardens within. And there are four other islands in the Galapagos Group—some smaller, some larger, than Cristobal—uninhabited and exactly similar in character. Nominally, they belong to Ecuador, which accounts for their tardy development; but here, surely, is a new field for enterprise.

In the midst of the valley, situated on a hillock and surrounded by the peons' grass houses, is the owner's *hacienda*. Here we met, at a dinner of strange but appetizing dishes, the accountant and the *comisario*, the former a rotund little gentleman with very long thumb nails (the insignia of the brain worker), which he clicked together with gusto when excited or amused; the latter a tall, handsome youth and something of an exquisite, if one may judge by biscuit-coloured silk socks and an esthetic tie.

It was a cheerful occasion, followed by the best coffee I have ever tasted and songs to a guitar accompaniment.

Out in the compound, under the stars, the peons also indulged in a New Year's *fiesta*; so that by midnight the place was a blur of tobacco smoke, oil flares, thrumming guitars; gyrating, brightly hued ponchos, with their owners somewhere inside them; dogs, chickens, and children.

Everyone seemed thoroughly happy and contented. And after all, what else matters? That is the Ecuadorean point of view, and who shall say it is a bad one?

A starlit ride to the beach, a few strokes of the oars that carve deep caverns of phosphorescent light in the inky waters, and we are again aboard. And herein lies one of the manifold joys of one's own ship. One may travel at will over the highway of the earth, carrying his home and his banal but treasured belongings with him. Like the hermit-crab, he may emerge where and when he will, take a glimpse at life thereabouts, and return to the comfort of accustomed surroundings—a pipe-rack ready to hand, a favourite book or picture placed just so.

Sheltered by a coral reef that broke the force of the Pacific rollers, and with holding-ground of firm white sand, we made up arrears of sleep that night, and scattered after breakfast to explore the beach.

There was a lagoon swarming with duck, not half a mile inland, that attracted Steve and his new twelve-bore gun like a magnet. Peter interviewed the lighthouse-keeper's wife anent cooking for us during our stay, and I—I lazed; it gives one time to notice things that escape the attention of the industrious.

A steam-engine was chugging somewhere behind the belt of stunted trees that fringed the beach, and I found it to be a coffee-grinder fuelled, if you please, with sawed lengths of lignum-vitæ—a furnace of wood at something like five dollars a stick in most countries! I should have liked to see the face of a block-maker of my acquaintance at such vandalism. But here it is nothing of the sort. Little else in the way of indigenous scrub grows on Cristobal.

Mechanically gravitating toward Dad's split-bamboo abode, I came upon him seated on a log, staring meditatively at the crumbling skeleton of what had been, or was at one time going to be, a ship.

"Why didn't you finish her?" I shouted into his "best" ear.

He stared at me in a daze, then burst forth in Spanish, until I succeeded in convincing him that he might as well talk double Dutch.

"Of course, of course," he muttered. "I forgot; Lord, how I forget! It's queer to me that I can speak English at all after all these years; but I can; that's something, isn't it?"

"Sure thing," I yelled; "keep it up. Tell me why you didn't finish your ship."

He pondered the matter; then spoke slowly:

"I told you of the other I built—and why. Well, I ran her on a reef—splinters in five minutes. Took the heart out of me for a bit, that did.

"Then I began to think of that loot again. I do still, for that matter; can't help it. You see, I think I know where it is. So I started on this one." He nodded toward the hulk, silhouetted against the crimsoning sky.

"I'd got to the planking when it occurred to me I'd want a partner for the job, at my age; and who could I trust? They'd slit your throat for ten dollars in those days. They murdered the present owner's father in cold blood. I wouldn't put it beyond 'em to do the same to this one if it wasn't that he's a smart lad and carries the only firearms on the island.

"No one's come here since, no one that I'd trust.... Then, too, what if I found the stuff? What good would it do me—now?" He spread out his delicately shaped hands in a deprecating gesture. "I should die in a month if I left here. Finest climate on earth, this is...." Suddenly he laughed—a low, reminiscent cackle of mirth.

"But that wasn't all that decided me. I'd got to the planking, Guayaquil oak it was, and I was steaming it on when a nail drew, and the plank caught me in the chest, knocked me six yards, and broke a rib. It's broken yet, I guess;

- 58 -

there was no one to mend it. Well, that finished it. I wasn't meant to build that ship."

He stopped abruptly and stared down at his battered rawhide shoes.

The inference was obvious.

"Well, what about it?" I suggested.

He looked up at that.

"I've been thinking about it ever since you came here," he confessed. "I'll go with you; but mind this, you mustn't curse me if nothing comes of it. I don't promise anything. All I say is I think I know where the stuff is, if someone hasn't got it."

"I'll let you know to-morrow," said I, and left him sitting there.

Was the man senile? There was nothing to make one think so. Was he a liar? There was equally nothing to prove it. At least half his story was a matter of island history.

We of the dream ship held a board meeting on the subject of loot that evening. We discussed it from every angle, and came to the conclusion that with the present atrocity called a motor auxiliary and the weather conditions of the group, we might take three days over the business and we might take three months; that the chances of finding something were outweighed by the risk of losing the ship, and that we were in pursuit of something visionary, anyway, so we had better get on with it.

The voting went two to one against, and I leave you to decide whose was the deciding voice.

I give this interview with Dad for what it is worth, and simply because I see no prospect of undertaking the search as it should be undertaken. I am aware that it reads like the purest romance, but it is true in every particular, as any one will soon discover on visiting Wreck Bay, Cristobal Island, in the Galapagos Group.

The old man still waits there on the beach for a ship and someone he can trust; but judging by his frail appearance (he is seventy-seven), he will not wait much longer.

Often during the days that followed I found myself standing at the dream ship's rail, looking seaward to a dim outline of mountains against the blue, and wondering.... But only the ash heap knows.

THE MARQUESAS ISLANDS

*The real South Seas—Big-game shooting
extraordinary—A case of thwarted ambition*

CHAPTER IX

*The real South Seas—Big-game shooting
extraordinary—A case of thwarted ambition*

We of the dream ship were "watering," or rather transferring, three hundred gallons of a doubtful-looking fluid from the beach reservoir of Cristobal to the ship's tanks by means of kerosene tins, a rickety landing-stage swarming with sand flies, and an equally rickety dinghy.

We were, in fact, enjoying a spell, to the accompaniment of vast quantities of cocoanut milk, before setting sail for the Marquesas, three thousand miles distant, and were in no mood for an interruption, which is probably why it came. A pigmy figure on the landing was apparently dancing a hornpipe and emitting strange cries.

"Who is it, and what the —— does he want?" I queried with customary amiability.

"It's the *comisario*," said Steve, with binocular upheld in one hand and a brimming cocoanut shell in the other, "and he's probably found that we need a bill of health or clearance or something."

I believe I sighed. I have a notion that Steve swore, and I am quite sure that we rowed ashore and interviewed the *comisario*, the handsome youth whose silk socks and passionate tie contrasted strangely with his surroundings. He still danced.

"He says that it is necessary that he should accompany us," Steve translated.

"To the Marquesas?"

"To anywhere."

"Really? And where does the necessity come in?"

After still further variations of the hornpipe and a prodigious outflow of Ecuadorean Spanish, the following was evolved: They were after him—a trifling indiscretion in the matter of issuing grog licenses to the peons. The Ecuadorean Government was to blame. They expected an official to live on twenty dollars a month and nothing else! How was it possible? Moreover, the President himself, elected on a wage basis of forty-dollars-a-month-and-bring-your-own-blankets, would be getting the boot in a short three months, and with him went everyone—everyone!

What was then to happen to the officials he had placed in power? More important still, what was to happen to this particular official? He must accompany us. It was the only possible solution. He would work. *Carramba,* how he would work! and for nothing but his passage to anywhere—anywhere!

Steve and I exchanged glances. The entire crew of the dream ship was, as I think I have before mentioned, exceedingly tired of cooking. The *comisario* seized on our silence.

Maybe we thought he could not work?

With a dramatic gesture he tore from his neck the passionate tie, from his feet the silk socks, from his back a virulently striped shirt, and stood revealed in a natty line of undervests.

"Poor devil!" said I, thinking of the dream ship's fo'c's'le in a seaway.

"Poor nothing!" said Steve. "He wants work; let him have it."

And that was how Señor ——, hereafter known as Bill, came to join the dream ship.

We sailed, and continued to sail before a steady southeast "trade" for twenty-two days, during which the *comisario* suffered alternately from seasickness, homesickness, and sheer inability to do anything but smoke cigarettes and sleep; our water tanks, under the magic wand of the Galapagos beach reservoir, transformed themselves into aquariums of energetic animalcules; and our entire biscuit supply crumbled to dust under the onslaughts of a particularly virulent red ant.

But these be incidentals to life aboard dream ships, and, at the first sight of Nukuhiva they faded to little more than amusing memories.

We had reached our goal! The South Sea Islands were ours! It was hard to realize. At the sight of gorgeous Nukuhiva gliding toward us over the sparkling blue water I remember looking round at the good old ship that had slowly but steadfastly carried us all these thousands of miles, and wondering what she thought of it all. I am aware that the idea of a ship having thoughts savours of senile decay, but that is what passed through my mind at the time, and has passed through it a hundred times since.

More nonsense has probably been written about the South Sea Islands than about any other part of the world. The library novelist, the globe-trotting journalist, and a reading public athirst for exotic romance have all contributed to this end: so that here, at the outset of attempting to describe what we of the dream ship saw there, I find myself at a loss. In short, "these few remarks" may be taken as an apology and a warning.

I have nothing to offer on a par with the standard article, such as struggles with sharks, conflicts with cannibals, or philandering with princesses. My line, I fear, is facts as I find them.

A fine island is Nukuhiva—as fine an example of volcanic formation as one will find anywhere. Sheer walls of cloud-capped rock six thousand feet high, some literally overhanging the crystal-clear water, and all embossed and engraved with strangely patterned basalt. There are pillars, battlements, turrets, so that with half-closed eyes it seems one is approaching a temple, a mediæval castle, a mosque of the East. And the valleys—deep, river-threaded, verdure-choked valleys fading away into mysterious purple mists. But it is little better than an impertinence to attempt a description of Nukuhiva after Melville's "Typee."*

*See Appendix.

For once the monstrosity in our engine-room was induced to exert three of its four cylinders, and we entered the harbour of Tai o Hae in style. It was as well, for a trim trading schooner flying the French flag was at anchor close inshore, and her entire crew lined the rail to see what manner of insect had invaded her privacy.

"Where are you from?" hailed a surprisingly English voice as soon as our anchor-chain had ceased its clamour.

"London," we chorused.

"Well, I'm damned!" came a response, evidently not intended for our ears, but audible nevertheless.

In rather less than three minutes a whaleboat-load of visitors was aboard the dream ship, and the silent bay echoed to a fusillade of question and counter-question.

Followed a dinner at the trading station on a wide, cool veranda, where, under the influence of oysters, California asparagus, fowl, bush pig, taro root, and French champagne, we became better acquainted with our hosts—two as amiable Frenchmen as ever I met. They represented a trading company of Papeete and Paris, and lived as only Frenchmen appear to know how to live.

The Marquesans, we gathered over coffee and cigars, were dying rapidly. Consumption. Introduced in the form of Panama fever by labourers returning from canal construction. The fever afterward developed into the white plague by reason of the natives' unresisting, if not acquiescent, nature. And when all were gone, what then? Chinese.

The Chinese appear to be the answer to most questions in the South Pacific to-day. They come; it costs them but fifty dollars to land; and after that they grow—*mon Dieu*, how they grow!

And can nothing be done? A shrug of the shoulders and the offer of a refilled glass are the answers of the Frenchman. But a short time now and he personally will be in a position to return to his beloved Paris, or Marseilles, or Brittany.

But we had lately returned from dealing with the Boche; so had our hosts. We drank respectively to the Royal Field Artillery, the Mitrailleurs, the Machine-gun Corps, and the incomparable French Infantry. What of it, if we continue the sport on the morrow, among the wild cattle and goats of Nukuhiva? To-morrow, then, at five o'clock.

The schooner, scheduled at daylight to load copra worth five hundred dollars a ton, was cheerfully detained for the trip, and loaded to capacity with bottled beer, coughing Marquesans, and a varied armoury of firearms.

We sailed down a coast that it is a sore temptation to describe and landed by whaleboat on a surf-pounded beach. Thereafter we plodded, crawled, and stumbled over as vicious a country as it is possible to imagine—crumbling shale, razor-edged ledges, and deceptive tableland of knee-high grass that only served to hide the carpet of keen-edged volcanic rocks beneath.

And the heat! But a representative of the incomparable infantry led the way; and who would not follow to the death, out of very shame? At each halting place the *élan* of this same representative seemed to increase. Sitting crosslegged on a rock in the meagre shade of a scrub tree, he would discourse on any subject under the sun, while his audience gasped, emptied the perspiration out of their boots, and cursed the *cantine* (a gigantic native bearing an almost as gigantic sack of bottled beer) for lagging.

I was under the impression that the game was to have been wild; hence my surprise when a herd of something like a hundred and fifty goats of all ages, from the bearded and maned veteran, or "stinker," down to the daintiest kid, cavorted up to our resting-place and sniffed at us inquisitively. It was necessary to fling stones to keep some of the more daring at bay.

So much for goat-hunting in the Marquesas. It is evident that these beasts are so "wild" that they know nothing of man; who shall say they have missed much in consequence?

The Dream Ship Passes from Atlantic to Pacific

At St. Lucia, West Indies

The Dream Ship Passes from Atlantic to Pacific;
At St. Lucia, West Indies

The cattle are a different matter. Shy as deer, they must be warily stalked and shot mostly on the run, at anything from a hundred to a hundred and fifty yards; also, they have an engaging habit of turning when wounded and giving the huntsman the worst possible time in their power, which in the case of a hefty bull or cow with calf is not inconsiderable.

Launching Outrigger Canoe in the Marquesas

Photo by Ralph Stock

Pascal, the Pearl-diving Non-starter

Launching Outrigger Canoe in the Marquesas;
Pascal, the Pearl-diving Non-starter

There must have been a herd of something like fifty grazing on the precipitous hillside, and the first shot, fired by an over-anxious Marquesan, against strict orders, sent them scuttling like antelope out of the valley and over the ridge. One fine bull received his medicine from my trusty little Winchester on the very brink, collapsed, and rolled like an avalanche of meat to the bottom.

We bagged four of this herd, and the Marquesans fell on them, quartering and selecting with extraordinary skill, and finally carrying one hundred pounds each of solid meat to the beach five miles below. How this last feat was accomplished by a band of ramping consumptives I have no notion, though I saw it done. I only know that after carrying two rifles and a gun over the same country I literally tumbled on to the beach, bruised and bleeding and trembling from sheer fatigue. Even the representative of incomparable infantry admitted to being tired, and, thank heaven, he looked it!

It had been a successful day, I was given to understand, and there followed in consequence song and dance aboard the dream ship until dawn touched the peaks of Tai o Hae.

A native dance is a dreary and monotonous affair to the average white man, because he does not take the trouble to understand. He sees before him an assembly of posturing, howling natives, and seldom realizes that he is witnessing a pageant of history that has never been written or read.

The performance opened with a pantomimic representation of the cruise of the dream ship. According to the actors' ideas, all aboard suffered acutely from seasickness, were utterly unable to stand upright, and continually looked for land under the shade of an upraised hand. Our vigour in battling with storms was extraordinary; we stumbled over rope-ends, clung to the rigging, nearly capsized, and one of us fell overboard, to be rescued, amid shrieks of laughter, by means of a boat-hook and the seat of his pants.

We were a joke, there was no doubt about that, and any one who takes a ten-thousand-mile journey in a twenty-three-ton yacht to the Marquesas and wants to be taken seriously had better go elsewhere.

From such trivialities the performers passed on to what was evidently their stock repertoire—the history of the Marquesas as handed down from father to son. It was all there in gesture and chant—mighty battles with their neighbours the Paumotans, cannibalism, peace, the advent of the white man with his rum, the plague that still consumes them, and all enacted without resentment.

That is the most astounding thing, that these people who were living their own lives, and surely as happy lives as ours, bear no ill will for the incredible sufferings our civilization has brought among them. Perhaps they do not think, and if so it is as well.

Conceive yourself, if you can, oh, denizen of Park Lane, Fifth Avenue, or Champs Elysées, a healthy, upstanding, unclad savage of-the South Seas, and living your own life.

You may be a cannibal; and are there no cannibals, and worse, west of Suez? You will be a warrior and fight for your country and your womenfolk. Is there anything wrong about that?

You will have a stricter moral code than most white folk, but that cannot be helped. You will hunt and fish and gather fruit for your family—in fact, you will live in the only way you know how to live, in contentment.

One day an extraordinary-looking object called a white man presents himself and informs you that you are not living in the right way at all. A much better way, according to this gentleman, is to exchange a ton of your cocoanuts for a bottle of rum or a death-dealing instrument made of rusty iron.

You are a tolerant sort of person, and you listen and drink his rum. The next day you have an insufferable headache, and, logically concluding that he has poisoned you, you kill him.

But that is not the end. Replicas of him keep arriving, and you find you need his rum and his rusty iron, the one for its elevating properties, the other for its dispatch in dealing with enemies. Still more replicas arrive, but of a different order. Many of them are kindly, well-meaning men, and great talkers. They tell you that they have found a God—the only God—and you must worship him in their way. The trouble is that each has a different way, but they are all right, and they all prove it by the same book.

Preserve me from the futilities of theological argument; but I met at Tai o Hae a Seventh Day Adventist missionary, an earnest, clean-living, kindly man, without a spark of humour in his composition. He was consumed by a genuine and mighty fervour to demonstrate to the native Marquesan that he was keeping the Sabbath on the wrong day.

"Does that matter so very much?" I asked him, and that was all I had a chance to ask. Apparently it did matter. And he was getting converts. Why? Because the native is not slow to discover that by embracing Seventh Day Adventism he gets two days of rest in the week.

Elsewhere I have met Roman Catholic, Mormon, Latter-Day Saint, Presbyterian, and Anglican Church missionaries, all at work in the same field, all earnest, well-meaning men, and each convinced that he is right.

Is it any wonder, then, that after listening to them all the dazed South Sea Island native asks himself what all the pother is about, and, finding no satisfactory answer to the conundrum, turns to his tangible rum bottle?

To revert to safer topics, there is pearl shell in the Marquesas. The representative of incomparable infantry told us so while we sat on his incomparable veranda one morning, consuming large quantities of *papia*, rolls, honey, and coffee, each in his particular brand of pyjamas.

The information brought upon our serene lives at Tai o Hae the white man's blight of avariciousness. Was this thing possible, with shell at one thousand dollars a ton delivered at Philadelphia? Yes; he, the incomparable, had seen it through a water-glass, in anything from five to fifteen fathoms, between the islands of Hivaoa and Tahuata.

Why had it not been prospected? It was doubtful if any but he and the natives knew of its existence. Undoubtedly it was worth looking into. He made us a present of the information to do with as we willed. His cook was an old Paumotan diver, who would no doubt accompany us—Pascal!—accompany us to the island, a bare ninety miles distant. We could take samples of shell to the company in Papeete, and no doubt make arrangements—Pascal!—arrangements with them to advance working capital in return for a lien on the shell—Pascal!!!

"Monsieur." An enormous Paumotan native stood in the doorway smiling benignly.

He would accompany us. He would cook, and he would dive.

We sailed that evening, the deck being littered with green bananas, live chickens tied by the leg to bulwark stanchions, a rabbit, firewood, a stove composed of a kerosene tin half filled with earth, and—Pascal.

There was apparently nothing this extraordinary man could not do. He knew every island of the Marquesas like the palm of his hand. He could produce savoury messes from a kerosene tin, remain under water three minutes, discourse entertainingly in pidgin-English, French, German, Marquesan, and Paumotan, and secure a ship's provisions without the annoying triviality of paying for them.

"But whom do we owe for all this?" I asked him, eyeing the menagerie that surrounded us.

Pascal smiled and waved a hand.

"Rabbit no money," he informed us; "chickens, bananas, all no money. Me get um."

Here surely is a solution of the high-cost-of-living problem. Take Pascal to the profiteering areas and the thing is done.

Dawn revealed to us Tahuata close abeam. Each island of this group seems more lovely than the last: waterfalls pouring three thousand feet to the sea, blow-holes at the base of rocky cliffs that spray the air with spindrift and miniature rainbows, deep bays with coral beaches at their head.

But the beauties of nature were not for us on this occasion; we were prospecting. It was a serious business. There might be money in it. After this

I can scarce believe that in Paradise itself the white man will not be dogged by the curse of opportunism.

Leaving the dream ship at anchor a cable's length from shore, we took to the dinghy and explored the floor of the ocean thereabouts through water-glasses, consisting of wooden boxes with glass bottoms. This was the place, Pascal informed us, and, sure enough, there was shell, old barnacle-encrusted shell, but widely scattered.

What of a few samples? Pascal grinned and shook his head. "Shark," he muttered, apologetically; which, being interpreted, meant that he refused to dive.

Men with water-glasses in boat

He pointed out that in the Paumotus it was different. In the Paumotus there was always a reef-surrounded lagoon where few sharks found entrance. In the Paumotus men dived in couples as a safeguard. In the Paumotus——

In vain we pointed out that we happened to be in the Marquesas and not the Paumotus; that he had been hired to dive in the Marquesas; that we were really very angry—in the Marquesas. He grinned.

A Man of the Atolls

Photo by Ralph Stock

A Man of the Atolls

In rather less than half an hour, and to Pascal's utter amazement, we had put him and his belongings ashore, paid him his wages, and were under way for Tahiti.

Ah, Monsieur of the incomparable infantry, I rather suspect you of pulling our legs. Or was it that your innate enthusiasm ran away with you? Or that we should have been less hasty? I do not know. All I know is that you spoke truth; there is shell in the Marquesas—and it is likely to remain there.

Off Nukuhiva, Marquesas Islands

Off Nukuhiva, Marquesas Islands

As the South Pacific Islands become more widely known, which they are rapidly doing, the Marquesas are bound to attract the attention they deserve. Apart from their scenic grandeur and healthful climate, they are as fertile a group as any in the Pacific, and more so than most. It has been proved that cotton of the best quality flourishes there, as well as sugar cane and every other tropical product, and there are thousands of acres of knee-high, well-watered pastures for the stockman.

Since this visit to the Marquesas I have been living in France, to which country the group belongs, and I have not yet met a Frenchman who knows of their existence. In fact, the average Frenchman's ignorance of his own possessions is nothing short of amazing.

Some day the congested areas of this queer old world will overflow, and the Marquesas will be discovered afresh. When that time comes, France will have people knocking at her door and demanding to know why she debars all other nationalities from acquiring land that she does not attempt to develop herself.

Already there is a movement afoot in England to establish a colony in the Marquesas. Permission has somehow been obtained from the French Government—a process comparable with the extraction of a particularly obstinate winkle from its shell—to purchase blocks of land, and distribute them amongst intending settlers who already number over a thousand.

"Lucky thousand!" say I, "and good luck to them!"

THE PAUMOTU ISLANDS

The people of the atolls—including Mr. Mumpus

CHAPTER X

The people of the atolls—including Mr. Mumpus

From the moment I first set eyes on an atoll it fascinated me, and its lure has not departed with the years.

Think of any place in the world that you have seen, and an atoll is different. It is the fairy ring of the sea. Out of the depths it comes, rearing a vegetation and people of its own, and often into the depths it goes, leaving no trace. How? Why? Scientists murmur something about the coral polyp; but, not being a scientist, I prefer my theory of the fairy ring. That was how it looked to me many years ago, and that was how it looked again from the masthead of the dream ship.

We had left the Marquesas seven days previously, and were now becalmed in that maze of atolls known as the Paumotu or Low Archipelago.

Imagine a circular beach of glistening coral sand and green vegetation from five to fifty yards wide, thrust up through the sea for all the world like a hedge, and enclosing a garden of coral fronds submerged under water so still and clear as to be hardly visible, and you have an atoll as I saw it from the masthead.

And there were myriads of them—big atolls, little atolls, fat and thin atolls—fading away into the shimmering heat haze of the horizon. The fairies must have been mighty busy down this way.

I descended to the deck and things mundane. What to do when becalmed in a network of coral reefs and seven-knot currents was the problem that confronted us. I had no text book on the subject, but by some miracle the monstrosity was persuaded to fire on two cylinders.

Imagine yourself, then, passing through the narrow gateway in the hedge—I should say, passage in the reef—and coming to anchor in the garden—I mean lagoon.

It is sunrise, and already the pearling canoes are putting out from the village and scurrying to the fishing grounds over the glassy surface of the lagoon.

A fine people, these of the atolls—upstanding, deep of chest, a race of mermen if ever there was one. From birth up, if they are not in the water they are on it or as close to it as they can get. Take them inland and they die. So they squat on their canoe outriggers, smoking, chatting, laughing, until the spirit moves them (nothing else will), and one of their number drops from sight, feet first, with hardly a ripple.

You look down and you see him, as though through green-tinted glass, crouched on the sloping floor of the lagoon. He is plucking oysters as one would gather flowers in a garden. There is no haste in his movements, nothing to indicate that there is any time limit to his remaining down there, under anything from five to fifteen fathoms of water.

A minute passes, two minutes; still he pursues his leisurely way, plucking to right and left and thrusting the shells into a network bag about his neck.

The man of the atolls is in a world of his own where none but his kind can follow, and they still squat on their outriggers, chatting and laughing like a crowd of boys at a swimming pool.

One alone seems interested in the diver's movements: his mate, a fair-skinned woman, with streaming blue-black hair, leans over the gunwale of the canoe, looking down through a kerosene tin water-glass.

The diver's dark figure against the pale-green coral becomes more blurred; a stream of silver air bubbles floats upward. Three minutes by the watch have come and gone. To the landsman it seems incredible; and even then there is no haste, no shooting to the surface and gasps for breath.

The dark body becomes clearer in outline as it emerges from the depths, and slowly, quite slowly, floats upward until a jet-black head breaks water and the diver clings to the gunwale of the canoe, inhaling deep but unhurried breaths and exhaling with a long-drawn whistle peculiarly his own.

In what way this whistle helps matters it is impossible to say, but whether a habit, a pose, or an aid in the regaining of breath, it is universal throughout the Paumotus; so much so that a busy afternoon with the pearlers sounds more like a tin-whistle band than anything else.

With the people of the atolls the ability to remain under water for long periods is more than an art; it is second nature. Instinctively, they do just those things that make one breath suffice for three minutes and sometimes four.

Preparatory to a descent they do not take a deep breath and hold it until the surface is reached again. They fill their lungs with a normal amount of air, which lasts them about a minute and a half; the other minute and a half is occupied in its exhalation. Then, too, every movement below water is made with the utmost conservation of energy; yet a good diver can bring up a hundred and fifty kilos of shell in a day, which means in the neighbourhood of six hundred francs.

And it is just these same nimble francs that tempt the Paumotan to abase his talents, even as others are tempted the world over. For the sake of a few more shells, another cluster a little farther down, he remains below just that trifle longer than is good for him, and in time it tells. The eyes become bloodshot and start from the head, he goes deaf, or paralysis seizes him.

"But the women are the worst," a sun-baked trader informed me; "the worst or the best, as you like to put it," he added, grinning. "They'll go on till they burst, or pretty near it. Bargain-counter instinct, I guess. We call it the 'bends.'"

"'The bends?'"

"Yes, one of 'em goes down, and down; sees some more shell a bit lower, and some more a bit lower than that. Then she's reaching out for one last flutter at something like twenty fathoms when they get her the 'bends,' I mean. You can see her fighting against them, but it's no good; they bring her knees to her chin, and she can't straighten up, and she drops the last lot of shell she's gathered, and hates that worse than the 'bends'."

"What does she do?"

"Nothing, except lie there crumpled up until her mate fetches her up and massages her back to life. Then she's no sooner conscious than she's down again.

"Water never kills this crowd; it takes dry land to do that. Why, there's a diver close on fifty years old here, paralyzed clean down one side. He can't walk, but he can swim. He gets them to carry him down to the reef and heave him in; says it's the only place he can get any comfort."

"How about sharks?"

"Oh, there are sharks all right, but the diver's mate looks after that; gives the signal, and they're all in after him double quick."

"Finish him off with knives, eh?"

The sun-baked trader smiled reminiscently.

"Well, hardly," he said. "A dead shark makes a square meal for the others, and that's all. What they need is an example, and they get it. They're cruising about sometime when they come on one of their number with no tail, one fin, and sundry other decorations that wouldn't exactly please the S.P.C.A. He is not nice to look at, and they clear out of a place where such things are possible.

"When an island's thrown open for pearlings, we spend weeks mutilating sharks before the divers'll go down, and small blame to them, I say. Sharks are—well, sharks."

The casual reader picks up a good deal of information about "gold rushes" and such-like romantic undertakings from the plethora of novels on the subject; but who has ever heard of a pearl-rush? Yet they occur every year in the Paumotus.

The group belongs to the French, and is administered from the local seat of government at Papeete, Tahiti. Here a heterogeneous collection of humanity awaits the opening of the pearling season like a hovering cloud of mosquitoes.

There are pearl buyers from Paris and London, representatives of shell-buying concerns from Europe and America; British, Chinese, and Indian traders, speculative schooner skippers and supercargoes, not to mention the riff-raff of the beaches, all intent on pickings from the most prolific pearling islands in the South Pacific.

Shark, pearl diver

And this is the law of the group—infringed, circumvented, broken, but still the law—that although under French Government, the Paumotus and all they produce belong to the Paumotans.

Still further to protect the native, diving apparatus is banned throughout the group. The oyster, as he brings it from the water, is the diver's property. He must open the shell aboard his canoe before touching land, remove the flesh, and, after testing it for pearls (usually by kneading it so thoroughly between finger and thumb as to crush the life out of it), throw it back into the lagoon to propagate its species. Should he find a pearl, it is his also.

It is then up to the cloud of "mosquitoes" before mentioned to get both shell and pearl out of him as best it can. One can imagine the buzzing and biting that ensue.

From the buyer's point of view, the sooner and the deeper he gets a good diver into his debt the better. He then has some hold. Consequently, he spoon-feeds his selected divers like the infants that they are. Tinned delicacies of all sorts, Prince Albert suits of unbelievable thickness and cut, silk socks, and stockings are a good diver's for the asking during the closed season.

With shell at one thousand dollars a ton in Philadelphia (the largest consumer at the present time), and pearls soaring to apparently limitless heights, all will be well when work starts.

And the diver? From long experience of "mosquitoes," he is by no means slow. Shortly before the season opens he is presented with a bill that would cause most of us to register apoplexy. He looks at it, grins, and proceeds to dive. He also proceeds to make caches of shell on the floor of the lagoon, only bringing up half of what he collects in payment of his debts. At night he retrieves his cache and sells for cash to the smaller "mosquitoes" who infest the beach. As for pearls, from the moment the diver's finger and thumb encounter foreign matter in the flesh of the oyster, he becomes about as communicative on the subject as his catch. Should the truth leak out, his find will promptly be confiscated in payment of his everlasting debts, or the wily pearl-buyer will use threats of exposure to reduce the price.

No, the diver, if he is up to snuff, will work his passage to Papeete on a schooner, sell to a Chinaman, who neither asks questions nor tells tales, and proceed to enjoy himself according to his lights.

Blossoming into a Prince Albert suit, a red tie, and silk socks, he will hire a car, load it up with lady friends and execrable rum, and vanish into thin air for a fortnight, at the end of which time he has somehow contrived to get rid of all he possessed and is perfectly prepared to return to his atolls and his debts. He has lived like a white man and cheated the "mosquitoes"; what more can Paumotan heart desire?

The thing we call progress has slain the picturesque in most industries of this world, but not so with pearling in the Paumotus. During the season, the beach of one of these atolls resembles an Old-World fair more than anything I can call to mind.

A crazy merry-go-round brays and rocks in the shade of the palms, luring the adventurous to invest three pearl shells in a ride on a broken-necked camel. The ubiquitous movie "palace" has reared its unlovely head, and for more shell or five cocoanuts one may witness on the shores of a South Sea lagoon the battered remnants of a love affair enacted not far from Los Angeles. I have often wondered what happens to all the worn-out films in the world. Now I know.

This season, and for the first time, the people of the atolls are to be initiated into the mysteries of ice-cream. Truly, the "mosquito" stops at nothing.

It was down in this part of the world that I met Mr. Mumpus, though that is not his name. To reach him you must pick your way with the motor auxiliary through a maze of reefs, lie off and on, because there is no pass into his lagoon, and plod through blazing sand in a temperature of ninety in the shade, which there is not. But it is worth it.

You will probably find him in the pearl orchard, a green-lined umbrella in one hand and a dripping oyster shell in the other. He will stare fixedly at you for upward of half a minute and then say: "How the devil did you get here?" with a brusqueness that is alarming until you get used to it.

In my own case I indicated the dream ship, looking particularly smart in her recent coat of white paint.

"What! In that thing?" remarked Mr. Mumpus.

I was smitten to silence for a space.

"I heard you were making pearls," I told him on regaining something of my equanimity, "and thought you might be so good as to tell me about it."

"Come up to the house," he barked, and led the way to a rambling erection of corrugated iron and palm leaves containing, as far as I could make out, a gaping "boy" of uncertain origin, some empty soap boxes, and a microscope.

"There's nothing new in what I'm doing here," he told me over two brimming shells of cocoanut milk, "nothing that the Chinese have not been doing for centuries. The pearl is a disease of the oyster; introduce the disease and you will get a pearl."

"Quite," said I.

"No one has succeeded up to the present," continued Mr. Mumpus, "but there is no reason why it should not be done in time, no reason at all. I am appreciably nearer than I was a year ago, for instance. In the meantime, I am producing the ordinary blisters, or half pearls, with various foundations. You see, the cestoid———"

But I cannot hope to set down here all that this amazing man told me in scientific jargon, as he strode back and forth across his mat-strewn floor.

He was a doctor by profession, had tired of it, and come to the islands to pursue his hobby of pearl culture. He takes an oyster from the lagoon, opens it very carefully by the slow insertion of a wooden wedge, and places a pilule of beeswax against the main muscle. The mantle of the oyster then covers it with mother-of-pearl, and in the course of a few months our friend cuts from the shell a very fair imitation of a half pearl.

But, as most people are aware, the real pearl comes from the flesh of the oyster, and it is on the production of the genuine article that Mr. Mumpus centres his efforts. He breeds oysters in the lagoon and dissects them under the microscope for signs of the parasite that undoubtedly causes the pearl. He injects into the flesh of others all manner of foreign matter.

Down there on his speck of an atoll he treats the oyster as a surgeon treats an interesting case and—who knows?—some day there may burst upon an astonished world the name of a man who can make pearls, and that name will not be Mr. Mumpus.

PAPEETE, TAHITI

Tahiti: its pleasures and problems

CHAPTER XI

Tahiti: its pleasures and problems

Although the Paumotus fully deserve their subtitle of "Low Archipelago," they have a marked effect on the southeast winds that are so prevalent in these latitudes, and so much relied upon by sailing craft.

The law of the "trades" is simplicity itself, and as a matter of general interest is perhaps worthy of mention here.

"Fickle as the winds" is a synonym that does not apply at certain seasons and in certain areas, and these areas, through mariners' reports, have been definitely located and recorded in the British Admiralty and United States Hierographic Office wind charts. A schooner skipper may now lay a course from, say, San Francisco to Sydney, and know to within a couple of points from which direction the wind will come for the entire voyage. He will be careful to "hug the trades"—the northeast down to the Equator, and the southeast beyond—and the reason of these steadfast and accommodating winds is that the hot air of the Equator naturally rises, leaving a vacuum that the cooler airs of north and south rush in to fill.

The Paumotus, however, with the intense heat generated in their mighty lagoons, form a miniature Equator of their own, and completely disorganize the "trades" thereabouts, with the result that weather conditions between this group and the Societies are notoriously unreliable.

A greater contrast between two islands a bare forty-eight hours apart can hardly be imagined than between the last of the Paumotus with its coral reef invisible at ten miles, and the cloud-capped volcanic peaks of Tahiti. It is like approaching another world. It *is* another world.

At the pass in the barrier reef off Papeete, a genial French pilot took charge, and secured us the best berth in the harbour. Here the coral wall that forms the beach is so sheer that it is possible to make fast to the trunk of a flamboyant, as though to a bollard on a quay, and walk ashore on a gangplank—which we of the dream ship promptly did and dined in splendour at the best hotel.

With unaccustomed collars chafing our leathern necks, and perspiring freely under the burden of clothes after a régime of towel and sola topi, we consumed iced *vin rouge, poulet rôti* with salad, and omelette *à la maître d'hotel.* Papeete was a pleasant place in that hour. Indeed, Papeete is a pleasant place at any hour. It is the metropolis of the south-eastern Pacific islands, just as Honolulu is of the northeastern, attracting as varied an assortment of humanity as any in the world.

Here we have the planter of vanilla and cocoanuts, the trader in anything from copra to silk stockings, the pearl buyer, the schooner skipper, and the ubiquitous adventurer on their native heath—and under conditions to make it possible for each to live and prosper.

The French may be wrong from our iron-bound, Anglo-Saxon point of view, but they certainly have the knack of making life a more enjoyable affair under their administration than under any other at the present time.

It was at Papeete that we of the dream ship lost our cook. It may be remembered that in the Galapagos Islands, five thousand miles back on our tracks, we rescued an exquisite Ecuadorean Government official from a delicate position by christening him "Bill" and installing him in our culinary department, where he was expected to work his passage to Australia.

He proved to be an expert cigarette smoker and little more, so that when he approached us after the first night in Papeete and intimated that he found it "necessary" to leave, we were neither surprised nor pained.

Pearl-diver About to Descend   Photo by Ralph Stock

Pearl-diver About to Descend

And so you may see to this day Bill, of the biscuit-coloured socks and passionate tie, leaning gracefully over the soft-goods counter of a French store, extolling the virtues of a new line in underwear or gallantly escorting a bevy of Tahitian beauty to the movies of an evening.

Bill has found his niche in the scheme of things, and who can say more?

"If you manage to get past here without trouble aboard, you'll be the first yachting party to do it."

So spake that kindliest of men, the acting British Consul of Papeete, and although we of the dream ship were fortunate enough to succeed where others had failed, I recognize the truth of his words. Right down from Bligh of *Bounty* mutiny fame to the most recent of pleasure cruises there is a succession of enterprises that have found their quietus at Papeete. There is something peculiarly demoralizing about the place. It invites to a laxity of mind and muscle unequalled in the Pacific, which perhaps accounts for its fatal fascination.

Pearl-divers in a Paumotan Lagoon

Mr. Mumpus's Blisters

Photo by Ralph Stock

Pearl-divers in a Paumotan Lagoon;
Mr. Mumpus's Blisters

How everyone lives, including a goodly sprinkling of whites, is a mystery that intrigues. I know a man hereabouts living in a twelve-by-fourteen corrugated iron shed furnished with empty crates and kerosene tins. At any odd hour that he chances to awaken from a more or less permanent state of torpor, he lounges into town and pays the smaller stores a visit. He pays nothing else. Starting at one end of a counter, with its sample edibles outspread, he systematically talks and eats his way to the other, and by the time the process is complete he leaves with a parting *bon mot*, and a full stomach.

He is a type of the present-day beach-comber, hardly such a romantic figure as his prototype of the "good old days," but in his way interesting. His is the art of getting something for nothing, and who amongst us shall say he has never essayed the feat?

I cannot let this gentleman pass without enlarging upon him, if only to illustrate the mental processes by which a cultured man may descend to the status of a beach-comber.

He had never worked, and declared that he never would, both of which statements I could readily believe. Why should he work? To make a living? He has one without it. To make money for the mere sake of making money? Such a pastime did not attract him. To save himself from boredom? He was never bored. Were not sunsets and cloud effects, and all the strange living things of the beach (including store-keepers) provided for his entertainment? To retain his self-respect? Not at all. If others found it necessary to plan and strive in order to retain their self-respect, let them proceed! Personally, he did not find it necessary, that was all; and he fell to gouging his foul nails with a jackknife.

"Of course," I ventured to murmur, "there is self-respect *and* self-respect."

"Quite," he agreed, cheerfully.

But the man's real secret, the canker at the back of his diseased mind, was revealed to me—as I have no doubt it has been to many others—in the most startling fashion. Suddenly, and apropos of nothing either of us had said, he sprang to his feet and struck an attitude in front of the rusty hurricane lantern standing on an empty fruit crate.

"Do you notice anything?" he asked me.

All I noticed was an elderly gentleman, inclining to corpulence and baldness, with rather a fine profile terminating in a Vandyke beard, standing rigidly with folded arms and an air of imperiousness that struck me as out of place.

"You see no resemblance?" he suggested, incredulously.

I saw none in particular, and said so. He took his seat with an air of disappointment.

"Then perhaps I may help you," he said. "My mother was lady-in-waiting to Queen Victoria when King Edward was Prince of Wales. Does that convey anything to you?"

Naturally, it did, and I was forced to admit a resemblance that had escaped me.

Touched? Perhaps.

Taking this unworthy as the lowest rung of the white Tahitian social ladder, one comes next to the clerks of the larger stores, who, after a year or two with their firm, are marooned in charge of a trading station on some distant island at a wage that makes honesty and prosperity incompatible.

Then comes the store manager in crackling white drills and a luxuriant office, who welcomes you with a winning smile, and speeds you with a staggering bill; the schooner skipper, a genial soul possessed of an enviable independence that empowers him to tell his "owners" to go to the devil for three months of a hurricane season each year, the while his ship lies in port, and he disports himself and his latest yarn over variegated drinks on the balcony of the Bougainville Club; the French Government official, as awe-inspiring in business hours as he is charming out of them.

Island inhabitants

As for the natives, they are to-day a relic—rather a sad relic when one comes to think of it—of a once-superb race. White man's blight has descended upon them and they have withered like so many of their brothers throughout the milky-way of the Pacific.

When shall we learn that what may be one man's meat is another's poison, and refrain from attempting to instil our ideas of progress into a people on whom they have precisely the opposite effect? The answer is, "Never—so long as there is money in it."

But an additional rung must be added to our social ladder of Tahiti, and a sturdy rung at that. The half-caste—especially the French-Tahitian half-caste—is deservedly becoming a power in the land.

The accepted idea of him is that he retains in his composition all the failings of the white man and none of his virtues, but like so many accepted ideas it is entirely erroneous. He is a human being with the failings and virtues of any other, and there is not a doubt that he possesses a physical and mental virility that carries him further than most toward success in the tropics. He is usually extremely handsome, quietly mannered, and industrious, and the women of his species are among the most beautiful in the world.

Lastly there is the Chinaman; and the more one sees of this bland, uninterfering race, the more one is driven to the conclusion that he has come nearer to solving the riddle of existence than any other.

When Tahiti suffered one of its periodical awakenings to the fact that it must have plantation and road labour, it imported some thousands of Chinese. But what it failed to do was to specify on its indent the kind of Chinaman required, with the result that the majority turned out to be of the store-keeping class, and about as much use for road-making or copra-getting as a sick jelly-fish. Some stayed by the work for which they were intended, but many more, in their own insidious fashion, set up shop, and to-day wield a financial influence in Papeete second to none. "I'd sooner work for the Chinks," a white super-cargo told me. "You know where you are with them. They give you a square deal, expect a square deal from you, and if they don't get it, give you the boot without back-chat. They're not in an ever-lasting, all-fired hurry, either."

So here are one or two secrets of the Chinaman's success. Is it another that he will buy a pearl for no other purpose than to drink it pulverized in tea? Who can say? It is certain that *he* won't.

It was here in Papeete that I became a *garçon d'honneur*, at least, that is what I was told I was, though at the time I felt, and I am sure looked, like nothing on earth.

If it had not been for Liza I should never have suffered the indignity of transition from the semblance of a man to that of a stuffed and hustled dummy. But who can listen to the pleadings of a particularly attractive half-caste Tahitian by moonlight on the deck of a dream ship without surrender? I cannot.

It was explained to Peter, as intermediary, that she (Liza) needed an escort to her sister's wedding, and thought that I should lend an air of distinction to the proceedings. She had fallen in love with my particular brand of sola topi, and she thought me *très gentil*. I expect this settled the matter. In any case, at nine o'clock that night, arrayed as ordered, and securely wedged between Liza and one of her innumerable and attractive female relatives, I was conveyed, swift as Ford could fly, to the offices of the *Maire*, where I was dragged forth and pushed into position to form one of a long procession of youths and maidens, the former in white gloves and evening dress ties, the latter in frills.

From, then onward I have no clear recollection of how I came to be in the various places that I found myself. Liza managed it. Liza was the most efficient tug I had ever made fast to. Up a lane of giggling onlookers we trickled and, after the civil ceremony, down it again, to be whirled away to the church, where the same performance, with certain variations, was enacted. Then to the home of the bride, and incidentally of Liza, a palace of light and heat, music and movement, where I found solace in a life-saver before the tug again made fast and towed me in to "breakfast."

I had fancied the marriage complete, the knot irrevocably tied. Not so. We stood about a long table, our hands itching to descend on a glass of inviting champagne, while the native department of the ceremony, and to my mind the most impressive, was conducted by a venerable Tahitian, a relation of the bride's mother.

He spoke, and continued to speak, untroubled by the growing restlessness of his audience. Liza pouted, and whispered in my ear, from which I gathered that the speaker had not been invited, that his mere presence constituted an insult. I failed to see why a representative of one side of Liza's family should receive such scurvy treatment, but lacked the courage to say so, which is perhaps as well. Instead, I asked what he was saying, and elicited the following:

"It is old Tahitian custom—he should not be here! It is old Tahitian custom when you marry you have new name. He is telling new name which must be 'WIND'; and when they have children, they are to be more 'WIND'. He should not be here! There, it is finish; drink your champagne."

Which, ever obedient, I proceeded to do.

Followed dancing, a strange mixture of hula and fox-trot, until four o'clock of the morning, a farewell to Liza under the stars, and a somewhat clumsy boarding of the dream ship.

Such is present-day Papeete, a place of pleasure, interest, or profit, according to taste.

Fish-spearing on the Reef
Photo by Ralph Stock

Fish-spearing on the Reef

The main trouble in the Societies, as elsewhere in the Pacific islands, is scarcity of labour. Each group in this mighty ocean is struggling with the problem at the present time, and has not yet succeeded in reaching a solution. The native will not work. He does not believe in toiling for others when he is a self-supporting landlord himself, and, when you come to think of it, why should he? The Pacific Islands, ambitious for development, are consequently forced to turn for help to the more congested quarters of the globe, such as India and China, and herein lies the danger. The influx has already begun, and there is not a doubt that in time it will swell from a beneficial stream into an overwhelming flood unless ultimately returned to its source by a conduit of stringent legislation.

Moorea, the Land of the Lizard Men

Moorea Greets the Dream Ship

Moorea, the Land of the Lizard Men;
Moorea Greets the Dream Ship

We of the dream ship left the pleasures and problems of Papeete with regret, but succeeded in leaving with our ship's company intact, to the lasting wonder of our very good friend the British Consul—to whom salaams from a less salubrious clime.

THE ISLAND OF MOOREA

The land of the lizard men—Facts and fancies,
including a few horrors

CHAPTER XII

The land of the lizard men—Facts and fancies,
including a few horrors

Many an hour of quiet content had we of the dream ship spent while moored off Papeete, in watching the ever-changing beauties of Moorea, a bare fifteen miles distant.

Whether viewed in fair or foul weather, at sunrise or sunset, this island with its fantastic volcanic peaks and deep, mysterious valleys of purple haze attracts the eye of the dreamer like a magnet. What secrets lay hidden in those valleys? What might not be seen from the summit of those peaks? We determined to find out.

But first it was necessary to attend to things practical in the shape of our alleged auxiliary engine. It was perfectly possible, here in Papeete, to hire an expert to diagnose the trouble, but I had had my fill of "experts" the world over. They have an engaging habit of setting the contraption in motion by some happy accident, and declaring that "it is all right now," but never by any chance explaining to the harassed owner what was the matter with it. It is my belief that they do not know themselves. The only point on which they are all agreed is that the "expert" who preceded them "made an unholy mess of the job," and that if it had not been for themselves, it is doubtful if the engine would have ever run again. Moreover, their bill is usually in keeping with their modesty.

After a three-hour heart-to-heart consultation with the patient, I discovered, quite by accident and with Peter's hat pin, that the tiny air-vent in the screw-top of one of the carburetors was clogged. Consequently, when the top was screwed down, the air had no outlet and forced down the float. Hence a persistent flooding.

It sounds absurd. It was absurd, but that was the entire trouble, and the accidental insertion of the hat pin converted lifeless scrap-iron into the power that the dream ship had so often and so sorely needed during the past months.

I hear the "experts" laugh, but I solace myself with the remembrance of one of their number leaping on his hat in an effort to locate an equally trivial trouble in marine motor engines, and draw the moral that it is as well to carry sisters who use hat pins.

A few hours' sail brought us to Moorea, and one of the finest natural harbours in the South Pacific, where we were met by a plantation owner of our acquaintance in an outrigger canoe, and piloted through a tortuous reef channel to an anchorage of firm coral sand.

The entrance to this harbour is fully half a mile wide, so how the captain of a French gunboat contrived to pile his vessel securely on the reef is something of a mystery. It is said that he had dined "not wisely but too well" in Papeete, and was filled with *élan* to demonstrate how close a shave he could accomplish without cutting himself. And again, that he had been sent to bring back cattle, a mission that, as a naval officer, he so abhorred that he had done the deed deliberately.

In any case, there lies his craft, a fine old hulk, with the rollers rumbling and seething through her vitals; fit warning to the mariner who would toy with coral.

Such grim monuments to mischance, negligence, or deviltry litter the reefs of the Pacific; and what tales they could tell! I know of one on Middleton Reef, now used as a store ship for other possible victims, that was piled there on a lee shore during a south-west gale, and the bottom ripped clean out of her. For a week she lay half-submerged, her crew wading the decks knee-deep in water, and gazing over her sides or down through her hatches at the provisions scattered on the coral. There was water down there—fresh water in breakers and tanks, and food in tins that only needed block and tackle to hoist them up to the poop. But who would dive down and make the tackle fast? It meant almost certain death of an even more hideous kind than faced them as it was, and, unlike the orthodox romance, there were no heroic volunteers. The skipper was ready and willing, but he had his wife aboard who restrained him by swearing that if he did any such thing she would throw herself and their three-year-old daughter after him.

In all, they waited a week without food or water before the threatening attitude of the crew forced the skipper to make the attempt in spite of his wife's entreaties and threats. He dived; he made fast the tackle, but all of him that came to the surface was a severed leg, and the wife followed him with her child in her arms.

It is strange that a region of such beauty as the South Pacific Islands should be the favoured home of tragedy, but so it is. My very good friend the late Louis Becke, who probably knew these parts better than any man of his time, often bemoaned the fact that when choosing a theme for one of his incomparable tales of the South Seas, he could not paint true to life without finding tragedy peering at him from every corner. He claimed the cause of it to be that this sunny realm of bronze gods was never intended to be invaded by the white man, and there are few who, in all fairness, can differ with him.

Even on Moorea, the incomparable, we of the dream ship had not been ashore an hour before encountering a thing too ghastly to ponder on. It was a man with legs so immense that only the toes of the feet protruded beyond them. His neck was thicker than his head, and part of his anatomy he wheeled before him, covered with a *parieu*.

It was a case of elephantiasis, a common disease of the islands, but against a background of such loveliness seeming the more terrible.

Here was a shady, grass-grown beach road overhung with flamboyants, and bordered with crotons and flaming hibiscus; there a cocoanut plantation with its serried ranks of graceful palm trunks fading away into cool green distances like the pillars of a dimly lit temple; a brook, bustling through thickets, its banks carpeted with wondrous ferns and velvety moss—and here a tumble-down, deserted native house—rearing its battered head above a tangle of tropical vegetation. It had once been a home, and the land about it a prosperous banana patch. The first family that had occupied it had developed elephantiasis. A second and a third had met with the same fate, and now no one can be induced to live anywhere near the accursed spot. It is taboo.

Scientists claim they have discovered the germ of this dread disease in the mosquito, but many believe it to be in the earth, like that of tetanus.

But to revert to more pleasant subjects: legends still live on Moorea. It is the land of the lizard men, an agile race of dwarfs who lived on the inaccessible ledges of the mountain range, and descended periodically on the coast-dwellers, bearing off their wives and other valuables. They carried a short staff in either hand, giving them the appearance of lizards as they scrambled back to their fastnesses where none could follow.

To prove his words, the Moorean native of to-day will point out uniform rows of banana plants growing in clefts of rock amongst the clouds—the crops of the lizard men! How, otherwise, came they to be there? And he would be a wise man who could find the answer.

It is in these deep valleys, too, that ancient rites were performed, rites that were rigorously suppressed by the Government, but have survived until quite recent years. Indeed, white settlers assert that they are not entirely eradicated to this day. Tradition, religion, superstition, call it what you will, dies hard.

Men looking at mountain

In this connection it was my good fortune to meet a retired police officer who probably had more to do with the suppression of "witchery" in the Islands than any man living.

"It mostly began with long-pig," he told me. "Long-pig? Well, you know the Kanaka fashion of rolling bush pig in banana leaves and cooking it in the ground. Long-pig doesn't happen to be *pig*, that's all.

"And long-pig was enough for us. We broke up the party by marching the diners off in irons. But there were other things that had us beat. I've lain on my belly of a night, looking through a rat-hole in a native grass house, and seen some queer things: a war club stand on end, and dance on its own over the mats the length of the house. I'm no fool, but I'm darned if I could see how it was done. There was no harm in it, any more than there is in these

- 95 -

new-fangled séances where spooks blow trumpets and rattle tambourines; but with Kanakas it may lead to long-pig, and that's what we were after.

"Then again, we watched one place for close on a month, and at the end of it found nothing we could lay hands on, but something *I* sha'n't forget.

"There must have been close on a hundred Kanakas squatting round the walls of the house in stony silence, when a wind sprang up that nearly blew the roof off and yet never so much as stirred the leaves on the palms twenty yards away. It was still blowing when something dropped through the roof, and squatted on the mats in the middle of the house.

"There wasn't much light—there never is at these chivarees, but there was enough for me to see that whatever it was it was a leper. It wasn't all there. It wasn't the right shape, or colour, but it boomed out answers to questions that the others put to it, and, knowing the lingo, I listened. It was the usual business: So-and-so's father was all right, but hoped that his son would join him before long as he was a trifle lonely. And somebody else's brother was having the time of his life with a brand-new sailing canoe that was the fastest thing yet. And somebody else was going to die soon....

"Now, you can arrest a leper on suspicion, and I did my best, but I never got that one. He just went, and so did the others, though they made more of a fuss about it; and all the time that wind was blowing the hair of my head this way and that.

"Fake? Of course it was a fake, but clever at that. I never got the leper, and that 'somebody else' died all right, because I saw him. But then Kanakas are like that: they die to order...."

True, the foregoing is hearsay, but it is first-hand hearsay, and on the best possible authority.

The only other Island witchcraft that I have encountered and can vouch for personally is fire-walking, a well known Kanaka pastime. That natives can make a pit of stones white hot with burning brush-wood, and then walk bare-footed upon them for upward of two minutes, is not so wonderful to the skeptic who knows that they paint the soles of their feet with a secret preparation that is a non-conductor of heat. But the fact that they can lead a white man, whose feet are not so treated, over the same stones, is a "trick" that needs some explaining.

Then, there is the herb for the unfailing and harmless production of abortion; a preparation of such preservative powers that it will keep the human body for centuries; and an innumerable array of magic potions undreamed of in our philosophy. Undoubtedly the Islands have their secrets, as quaint and wonderful as any in darkest Africa, and some day—which I trust is not far off—I hope to "inquire more closely."

Our planter friends of Moorea appeared to lead a pleasant life. Theirs was a bachelor bungalow run by efficient house-boys, and set on the fringe of a palm grove overlooking a vista of sea and reef and mountain as beautiful as any in the Island—which means in the world.

They were growing vanilla, and, although Britishers, had chosen Moorea as the scene of their labours because they preferred French rule.

"The French don't mess you about like our own people," one of them informed us. "They're not anti-this and anti-that. They leave you alone, and I can tell you we appreciate it after visiting a few of our colony-governed colonies." He referred, of course, to the mandates given to Australia and New Zealand over certain groups of the South Pacific. "It's like giving a kid something to play with. He's bound to break it."

The other of our two hosts was engaged in a passage-at-arms with Peter, and I pitied him. Trust a woman for either kindling or dousing a flame of enthusiasm in the male breast. But as she still holds to her viewpoint, and the question at issue involves every white woman who contemplates living in the South Sea Islands, it is of interest, and I take the liberty—and the risk—of quoting from her diary:

"One of them (our hosts) was engaged to an English girl of eighteen, and was going to send for her in a month or two, but expected opposition from her parents, who thought the Society Islands too uncivilized and out of the world for a young girl to be happy in. I must say I agreed with them.

"Perhaps for the first few months the novelty would keep her amused; but after that! I cannot imagine an intelligent, energetic girl being content to live her life on an island, however beautiful, where she would be the only white woman.

"I said something of the sort to her fiancé, since he asked my opinion. He said he had promised her a horse, as she was intensely keen on riding. Even then it meant that she would have to keep to the track which ran round the island, and one soon wearies of the same ride day after day, when there is no object in view but exercise.

"I suggested that she might help on the plantation, and that perhaps making things for her new home would keep her occupied, but was told it would be impossible for her to do a hand's tap of manual work as she would lose prestige with the natives (awful thought!) and that she was not the sort to like needlework or housekeeping as she was too much of a sport; besides, the 'boys' would do the latter.

"Then what would be left for the poor girl to do? I asked.

"'Oh, she could potter about; and then *I* should always be on hand,' was the reply.

"What could be said to a man who thought along those lines?"

The answer is an echo—"What?"

But I must confess to a sneaking sympathy for him, all the same. The position of the white man living alone amongst natives is difficult enough in all conscience, and any one who has done it will testify to the absolute necessity of retaining prestige. To lose it *is* an "awful thought!" for without it the white man sinks lower than his neighbours, and is soon regarded by them with unveiled contempt.

No; call it "bluff," what you will, but the white man cannot afford to part with his prestige. And how much more is it necessary when he has his womenfolk to protect?

In any case, the Islands are not a suitable home for white women, say what they will. There are isolated instances of them thriving there, but in the vast majority of cases they fall victims to a pernicious type of anæmia which, even if it does not kill, remains with them for the rest of their lives. And as for children, they thrive for about five years from birth, and then fade to mere weeds unless sent to more temperate climes.

Perhaps—who knows?—these things are but another proof that we harbingers of progress were not intended to invade the sanctuary of the South Seas.

PALMERSTON ISLAND

A hint of hurricane—The atoll of perfection,
introducing "Mister Masters himself"

CHAPTER XIII

A hint of hurricane.—The atoll of perfection,
introducing "Mister Masters himself"

Between the Societies and Australia there is a regular line of steamships calling at Raratonga, Samoa, and New Zealand, and it was to avoid this cut-and-dried route that we of the dream ship headed for Palmerston Island, a mere speck on the chart six hundred miles distant.

But we sailed just that trifle too soon that makes all the difference between a fair-weather passage and the reverse. December to April, inclusive, is the hurricane season in this part of the Pacific, when the schooner skippers from Raratonga and other places in the direct path of the cyclonic disturbance see fit to lie up in the comparative safety of Papeete harbour, and we sailed early in the latter month.

I am not claiming that we encountered a hurricane; far from it, for it is doubtful if even the dream ship would have survived a full-fledged demon of the species. In these same latitudes I have seen turf torn from the face of the earth and rolled up like a carpet by sheer force of wind, and mile-wide swaths cut as cleanly as with a sickle through settlement, plantation, and jungle. But these exhibitions of ferocity were witnessed from terra firma. It is a totally different thing from the deck of a small boat at sea.

Surely, if man does not recognize his own insignificance when faced with overwhelming turmoil of wind and wave, he never will. He shrivels on the instant from a being of considerable importance in his own estimation to the semblance of a microbe; and his craft follows suit by dwindling from a sturdy home to a cockleshell. That is why it is best for the mariner, if he can manage it, not to think too deeply during time of stress.

The demon was about, as evidenced by the barometer which fell to twenty-nine, but his main body, writhing in a circle as is his wont, must have missed us, for all we of the dream ship encountered was a lashing of his tail.

It was enough. It blew, and it rained. Lord, how it blew and rained! first from dead ahead, which caused us to heave to; then, as the vicious circle was completed, from dead aft, so that we "ran" like a wind-driven rag under double reef and storm jib.

It is an easy thing to "run"; the difficulty is to know when to stop. There is always the possibility of being "pooped," which simply means being overtaken by a mountain of water and crushed into the depths out of harm's way for good and all. To the uninitiated it would appear that the faster a ship travels the better chance she has of escaping a following sea. But this is not so. No one has yet succeeded in explaining the phenomenon satisfactorily, but it seems that the wake caused by even a small boat passing down the face of a comber induces it to break prematurely, and if the boat and the comber chance to be travelling at the same speed, the latter breaks aboard, that is all.

It is a chance that all who go down to the sea in ships must take when they "run," and the only way of obviating the disaster is to restrain a very natural desire to "get on with it" while the weather is fair, and heave to in time.

In the case of the dream ship there was no need to do this, as we had reduced canvas to such an extent that she was not doing more than ten knots, and rose to the summit of each breaking comber like a cork. I have yet to see the weather that she could not face without flinching, and I treasure her design beyond price.

After such a bucketing Palmerston was a welcome sight, as welcome as it was unique. It is doubtful if such another gem adorns the earth. Neither atoll nor island, it is a perfect combination of both; a natural necklace of surf-pounded coral strung with six equidistant, verdant islets, the whole enclosing a shallow lagoon slashed with unbelievable colour.

Men in boats

Such was Palmerston as we approached it before a stiff southeast "trade," to be welcomed by a fleet of amazingly fast luggers and their astonished crews.

Who were we?

Where had we sprung from?

Had we any matches?

To our own astonishment the questions were fired at us in English, and, what was more, English of a strangely familiar pattern. It is a quaint thing to hear one's own tongue fluently bandied amongst a brown-skinned people on an isolated speck of earth in mid-Pacific. But there was no opportunity of solving the riddle just then.

The Leaning Palms

The Leaning Palms

"Let go!"

"She's set!"

"Lower the peak!"

"Lower the main!"

The dream ship had come to anchor on the north-west side of the reef, well sheltered from the almost eternal southeast trades of these latitudes, and the pilot, a six-foot figure of bronze sketchily attired in a converted flour sack, was addressing us with a courtesy as unusual as it was refreshing.

Landing on Palmerston Island

Landing on Palmerston Island

With our permission, he would take us ashore at once. Mister Masters himself had given instructions.

The "Mister Masters himself" settled it. We tumbled into one of the luggers, tumbled out again at the reef, and stood knee-deep in swirling waters while the pilot and his crew towed the craft against a ten-knot current through the boat passage; then aboard once more and away at an eight-knot clip through a maze of coral mushrooms, bumping, grazing, ricocheting, until finally sliding to rest on a glistening coral beach.

"Mister Masters himself," a dignified old gentleman with a flowing white beard, a tight alpaca jacket, and the general air of a patriarch, met us at the veranda steps of his spacious home, and inside of ten minutes we were sitting down to a meal of meals.

Our host informed us that the schooner was overdue and we must excuse the viands, but I saw no need for apology. In fact, how a few acres of powdered coral could have produced the variety of edibles we consumed at that meal passes my understanding. "Sailing Directions" in its own terse way, says of these atolls: "Inhabitants live entirely on cocoanuts and fish," and it sounds stringent enough, but I beg to state that our menu on one of them, namely Palmerston, read as follows:

SOUP:
TURTLE

(Made of the genuine article, taken but a few hours ago from its playground in a zinc bath at the door.)

FISH

(I know not of what species, but tastier than most of the tropical varieties.)

BOILED FOWL

(And not the wretched victim of malnutrition emanating from most tropical barnyards; nor served undecapitated as appears usual in the Islands.)

ROAST PORK

(Which must have subsisted during its lifetime on something more nourishing than coral.)

VEGETABLES:
SWEET POTATOES
TARO ROOT

SWEETS:
COCOANUT PUDDING

(The core of cocoanuts stewed in milk squeezed from the meat of the nut, a dainty warranted to send the restaurant connoisseur into ecstasies if it ever reaches him, which is unlikely.)

Over rum, emanating from the dream ship, as the local supply of liqueur was retained for strictly medicinal purposes, the history of Palmerston Island was unfolded.

What any student of Island history knows is that it was discovered by Captain Cook in 1774 on his second voyage, though some authorities claim it to be the "San Pablo" of Magellan, the first island discovered in the South Seas; that on his third and last voyage Cook landed again to get fodder for his starving cattle; and that later on it came under the critical notice of the *Bounty* mutineers, who, after a thorough spoiling in luxurious Tahiti, decided against Palmerston as their future home.

But what everyone does not know is the history of the Masters family who now occupy the island.

One William Masters, as fine an old English sea-dog as ever came off a whaler, took a fancy to the place in 1862, leased it from the British Government, and, not believing in half measures, took unto himself three native wives. By each he had a large and healthy family that he reared in strict accordance with his own standards of social usage.

That they were sound standards is evidenced in the people of Palmerston to-day. They read, write, and speak English, this last with an accent vaguely reminiscent of the southwest of England. They are courteous, hospitable, and honest to a degree little short of startling these days, and although naturally inbred, they do not show it mentally or physically.

The islets scattered round the reef have been equally distributed amongst the descendants of William Masters's three wives, who now number ninety-eight, and under the authority of the island council, presided over by "Mister Masters himself," are worked to such purpose that they produce a thousand pounds' worth of copra per year.

I have Palmerston securely pigeon-holed in my own mind as the spot of all others in which, when the time comes, to sit down and wait for the end. The outside world, in the shape of a schooner from the Cook Group, intrudes itself but once a year. The ordinary infirmities to which flesh is heir are non-existent. The lagoon and the neighbouring islets are a mine of interest to the naturalist or sportsman, and the people have a charm that is all their own.

One thing alone troubles the Masters of to-day. To whom do they and their island belong? The war has changed all things. The Cook Group, two hundred and seventy-three miles to the southeast, of which Palmerston has now been declared a far-flung unit, is administered by New Zealand. Is "Mister Masters himself" to be taxed, governed, and generally harried by a people who hardly existed when his father took over the island? It looks like it. Here is as fine an example of the communal system worked out on a practical and prosperous basis as will be found in the world to-day. Why, and again why, cannot incipient administrators be induced to leave well alone?

A tour of the tiny settlement is worth while. Not long ago a French brigantine rammed the reef on a clear night of stars, while the crew, including the lookout, was below playing cards, with the result that Palmerston settlement to-day is for the most part built of ship's timbers and planking, companions, portholes, bunks, and miscellaneous brass fittings.

The little church, which is in course of construction and meantime serves as a school house, boasts walls and pulpit composed entirely of panelled doors from the hulk; and fine old seasoned timber it is.

The recognized playground is outside the church door under the palms, where a cricket pitch entices all and sundry. But the real playground of Palmerston is the boat passage in the reef, through which a mill race rushes at each turn of the tide. Here the multitudinous offspring of William Masters disport themselves on every contrivance that floats, from a full-fledged sailing-boat to a weather-board, and at the rate of knots sweep yelling round tortuous curves to or from the sea.

The dream ship, riding at anchor outside the reef, became the centre of attraction, and finally added to her many accomplishments by becoming a bargain store.

It may be remembered that on setting out from England we had laid in certain commodities known as "barter." Well, they were still aboard—slightly mildewed, but aboard—for the good and sufficient reason that we had not been able to get rid of them. It appeared that our ideas on the subject of "barter" were archaic. Nothing short of silk stockings, real gold watch chains, gramaphones, and gin is acceptable in the Islands these days. How could we offer such a discriminating public rusty jew's-harps?

But here was an opportunity not to be missed. "Sale! Sale!! Sale!!! Heart-rending reductions!" was the notice I suggested nailing to the mast, but there was no need. The entire population of Palmerston tumbled aboard like an avalanche, and gigglingly surveyed our effects outspread on the engine-room hatch.

To any one requiring the services of a thoroughly efficient window-dresser and salesman, I can heartily recommend Steve. Until the occasion of the dream ship's jumble sale I had, it appears, misjudged the man. Prose poems to a piece of voile (double width, slightly soiled and cunningly displayed on an arm) fell from his lips like rain. Imitation leather belts, looking glasses conveying a somewhat distorted reflection, near tortoise-shell haircombs, rusty knives, even jew's-harps, each and all possessed some sterling virtue of which I had been ignorant until enlightened by Steve. And they "went." It was my humble duty to make a note of the sales, and there was no keeping tally of them. In twenty minutes our "counters" were bare, and our customers clamouring for more.

And this was not all. From below, where Peter was supposed to be conducting a kind of ice-cream social without the ice-cream, came the unmistakable sounds of "barter," and when we mere males had succeeded in fighting our way through a solid mass of femininity, it was to behold her surrounded with a drift of every domestic commodity from raspberry jam to a safety-pin.

"They wanted them so badly, poor things," she confessed to me after the fracas, but did not succeed in hiding from me the embers of battle in her eye. Brothers are awkward things.

The National Sport at Palmerston Island—Shooting the Pass

Dragging a Boat through the Reef Pass

The National Sport at Palmerston Island—Shooting the Pass; Dragging a Boat through the Reef Pass

It was only when the last boatload of cheerful humanity had taken its departure, and we of the dream ship were dividing the spoils, that it was discovered by a closer reference to the invoices we had sold everything at *cost!*

Four more days we spent at Palmerston for the simple reason that we could not tear ourselves away.

It was a pleasant thing of an evening to wander over the firm wet sand of the beaches hand in hand with singing children, while a tribe of dogs leapt after mocking sea birds, or splashed into rock-pools snapping at the fish.

The Taro Patch   *Photo by Ralph Stock*

The Taro Patch

Perhaps the tide had turned, and one by one the coral mushrooms reared fantastic shapes out of the still waters of the lagoon—a gambolling elf, a ship under full sail, a mammoth bird or beast. It was difficult to realize one was not in fairyland—and an unworthy task at that. But again, even here, there entered the tragic touch of the South Seas. A thin spiral of blue smoke rose from the smallest of the islets across the lagoon, and I asked who lived there. A brother and sister, I was told, lepers.

"We're going to have shell in the lagoon as soon as we can get some by the schooner," "Mister Masters himself" told me on the veranda one evening. "Ought to do well enough. And we could run a few cattle here, too. But a schooner a year isn't much good to a man, is it?"

I admitted that it could hardly be called a "service."

"I'd have a proper passage dynamited in the reef," he went on, presently, "and you could do a bit of trading between here and the Cooks and Tahiti.

And you could have a house here, and Matha to look after you—if you'd care to stay."

I looked at him, at Palmerston, at the dream ship, and regretfully shook my head.

"Not yet," said I.

Au revoir, little island. Some day in the not very distant future a decrepit, irritable old man will return to your hospitable shores in search of peace; and if you are then as you are now—which Heaven send!—he will assuredly find it.

SAVAGE ISLAND

The Island called "Savage" including the ordeal by
Hospitality

CHAPTER XIV

The Island called "Savage," including the ordeal by
Hospitality

When Captain Cook discovered Niué in 1774, he christened it "Savage Island," and went on his adventurous way without landing because of the ferocious appearance and demeanour of the natives.

They, poor fellows, protest to this day that the great navigator's title is a misnomer, that they have ever been as peaceful a folk as any in the South Seas, and that the true cause of their ancestors' objection to a landing-party was their fear of white men's diseases, of which they had heard painful accounts.

We of the dream ship could sympathize with both parties. On the one hand, the track of infection is scored deep across the fair face of the Pacific, and on the other we had never beheld such a villainous-looking horde of natives as came to greet us at Niué. There were hundreds of them, each in a remarkably seaworthy type of dugout canoe painted black, so that the whole resembled a mammoth shoal of porpoises as they leapt from wave to wave.

This, however, is where the resemblance ended, for the porpoise is a sleek and silent gentleman, and the Niuéan is anything but that. He catches sight of a dream ship gliding slowly along his coasts under power, hurls himself into his canoe and paddles, yelling like a maniac, in her wake. He then rears himself on end, waves his paddle, and yells some more. By Herculean efforts he gains on her, comes alongside, grins malevolently, and yells into one's very face.

No wonder Captain Cook thought better of his shore-leave.

Yet when one comes to know these people better, as we of the dream ship did during the ensuing week, they are the most inoffensive, good-natured, open-hearted creatures imaginable. This naval reception was their idea of a really touching welcome. They were glad to see us—they are glad to see any one on Niué. Appearances are against them, that is all.

No sooner had we dropped hook at Alofi, the deepest bay around this iron-bound coast, than we were boarded by three gentlemen of a magnificence, in their crisp white drills, that put us to shame. But we of the dream ship had suffered this type of indignity so often that we were used to it. Besides, the magnificence of our visitors was happily only external, though they proved to be the Resident Commissioner, the Judge of the High Court, the Judge of the Native Land Court, the Collector of Customs, and the Postmaster; the Registrar of Courts and the Registrar of Births, Deaths, and Marriages; and the Chief Medical Officer.

Boat at island

Although, as I have said, there were only three of them, that is what they were, and you must separate them by the semicolons. Clearly they do not believe in overstaffing on Niué.

The first glad news to reach our ears was that we had missed a hurricane by three days. Oh, yes, Niué had them occasionally, and before now had been swept bare, but this particular one had passed like a ravening beast a few miles to the eastward. Had we seen or heard nothing of it?

We shook our heads in infinitely grateful negation, and the Postmaster—I beg his pardon, the Commissioner—exchanged a thoughtful glance with the Chief Medical Officer whom, it is to be feared, we had already christened "Doc." They had asked because the Cook-Group schooner that visited Niué with the unprecedented frequency of five times a year was considerably overdue. But we must come and live ashore; there was Government House, and the Law Courts, and the Gaol to spread ourselves over at a pinch.

And that was how we of the dream ship came to be so royally treated on Savage Island.

Legend has it that a great god of the past, with one foot firmly planted in the Tonga Group and the other on Raratonga, took it into his head to lift Niué out of the sea, and one can almost believe it. It is of weird formation, known scientifically as "upheave coral," and consists of two terraces, the lower ninety feet above sea level, and the other, two hundred and twenty feet, the intervening space being slashed with deep chasms. In short, Niué is nothing more than an atoll hurled bodily out of the sea by some mighty convulsion of the earth's past. One can clearly see that what was once the reef is now a mighty cliff and that the lagoon inside it is now a coral basin, pitched high and dry.

And this hybrid of an island is wonderfully fertile. On the terrace, that I cannot help looking upon as the reef, cocoanuts, bananas, and most other tropical products grow to perfection, while the lagoon—I should say valley— is thickly timbered with ebony and other hard woods. How came they to be there, considering they were never planted by human hand? Perhaps the Island Hercules who dragged the atoll from the sea saw fit also to cover its nakedness. No other solution of the problem presents itself.

"It's a queer spot," I was told during a motor tour of the Island by what is called "road," though it more closely resembles a coral switchback—"as queer as its people until you come to know them. But try and remember yourself at the age of thirteen, and you have the average adult Kanaka. Several of them joined up voluntarily with the Maori contingent during the war, and wear service ribbons in their hair if they can find no other place for them.

"Disease is our great trouble. The Niuéan has always been a born wanderer, and he brings things back with him; but we're getting it under by keeping them at home, and making failure to report a penal offence. They've always been hard workers, too. We planted fifteen thousand nuts on Armistice Day, and away back this was a favourite hunting ground for 'black-birders' on account of the Niuéan's appetite for toil. Bully Hayes, the well-known South Sea buccaneer, used to come here often, and, when he couldn't get men, took women—cargoes of them—to sell down in the leisure-loving Societies.

"Those? Graves. They've always buried their dead alongside the tracks, and we saw no reason to interfere. Good grave, coral, like a sponge—everything into the sea in no time. On top? Oh, that may be anything from a canoe to a pair of old boots. They have the same idea of 'laying the table' with the deceased's personal belongings as so many others. I nearly stole one of them once. It was a perfectly good sewing-machine, and my wife had nothing to run up curtains and things with when we came here. But I thought better of it. You have to go warily with these gentry."

At this juncture the long-suffering car plunged axle-deep into a quagmire of disintegrated coral, and refused to emerge until an army of Niuéans— advancing on us like a devastating host—attached themselves to its various parts and, by sheer manpower accompanied with indispensable yelling, dragged it forth.

Mr. Masters himself (with beard) boards the Dream Ship

Photo by Ralph Stock

Mr. Masters himself (with beard) boards the Dream Ship

We were close to a village, and the *piea* makers were at work. As a sidelight on the painstaking industry of these people, their preparation of arrowroot for food is illuminating. In an age when machinery does everything but—I was going to say "talk," but correct myself advisedly—it is a lesson in certain virtues that we of to-day seem to have mislaid.

The Dream Ship Bargain Sale

The Dream Ship Bargain Sale

Only one family works at a time, and brings its own implements. A stretch of coral sand is selected, and staffed with men, women, and children. The old women scrape off the discoloured rind of the roots with splintered cocoanut shell and throw them into a palm-leaf basket which the children rinse in salt water and carry to the men. They in turn grate the root into a coarse powder with instruments made of cylindrical-shaped pieces of wood bound at intervals with sinnet, the powder falling on to finely woven mats which are carried away by girls and tipped into a cradle of bamboo and cocoanut-fibre. This acts as a filter, through which salt water is poured while a man kneads the powder into a dough with such energy that he has to be relieved at frequent intervals.

The white spectators, if any, are then politely requested to retire while the final process of kneading and washing in fresh water is in progress, as it has been satisfactorily established that their mere glance turns *piea* sour.

Not wishing to dispute the fact, we complied—with the exception of Mrs. Commissioner's little girl, who had long cherished a desire to see the forbidden rite. Peering from behind a coral boulder, she was caught in the act and chased headlong and crying with fright before a shower of stones, to be comforted by her mother but severely reprimanded by the Commissioner, who is very rightly a stickler for etiquette where "his people" are concerned.

In these matters of form, convention, tradition—call it what you will—we of the outside world are inclined to imagine that we hold a monopoly, but such is far from being the case. The average South Sea Islander's codes are as numerous as, and far stricter than, ours, and when we deign to visit him with our particular brand of etiquette, and leave with the notion that we have in any way impressed him with our superiority, we make a vast mistake.

Inwardly (it is to be hoped), it causes us considerable amusement to note the "quaint customs of a picturesque people," but how often does it occur to us that our own antics are equally ludicrous to them, and that we are at a disadvantage in that our hosts are invariably too polite to show by word or look that we have infringed their code of ethics?

In this respect I have always remembered a visitor to China who was consumed with uncontrollable mirth at the spectacle of chop-sticks in action, the while he proceeded to fill himself with his knife.

Peter informed me that the chief trial she endured while moving in savage circles where it is impossible to converse was the necessity of wearing a more or less permanent smile; and I sympathized. We were in good company, for I believe Royalty is afflicted in the same way. But when you come to think of it, what else can you do with your face when confronted with a stonily staring multitude that you wish to impress with the fact that you are having a good time? It is a problem, the only solution of which to my mind is to carry a cheerfully expressioned mask, and don it as occasion demands.

Mrs. "Doc" had given up going with her husband on his rounds for this very reason. She said she found herself after a tour of inspection carrying a stationary smirk into private life, and it frightened her.

An occasion for the mask of appreciation, if we had chanced to carry one aboard the dream ship, presented itself the following evening. The paramount Chief of Niué very kindly invited us to a feast, and after consuming inordinate quantities of filling food, we sat, and continued to sit, while our host delivered an oration very ably translated by a pupil teacher from the mission school:

The paramount Chief of Niué, misnamed Savage Island, was overwhelmed by the honour we had done him in choosing his little island to visit—we who were used to the beauties and luxuries of the great outside. We must be brave warriors to cross so many miles of tempestuous ocean in order to see him and his people [the mask of modesty, please!]. Our ship, too, though small, must have been built by great artisans to have carried us so far and so safely.... When we returned, would we describe to the great King all that we had seen on Niué, and convey to him the loyalty of his subjects?

It was a neat speech, calling for a neat answer which, unfortunately, I have ever been incapable of supplying. But there was always Steve. After his unrivalled exhibition at the dream ship's jumble sale he was "called upon" by frenzied nudges in the ribs, and the confidence was not misplaced. Exactly what the dream ship would have done without Steve, I tremble to think.

Thursday Island Pearling Luggers

Thursday Island Pearling Luggers

The after-dinner speeches disposed of, Peter, in a confessedly comatose condition owing to a super-abundance of heat and food, yet with her own particular brand of smile securely in place, came in for special attention. The ladies of Niué do not speak; they act. The paramount Chieftainess advanced upon her with a beautifully woven hat in one hand, and with the other attempted to rid her of her existing headgear. Unfortunately, and amidst general consternation, it failed to come adrift on account of the pins, but this was soon remedied, and the gift securely wedged into place amidst loud applause.

Time was when the Niuéans were the best hat-makers in the South Seas, but with the introduction of the Panama their product has fallen into disrepute. It is hoped by acclimatizing the Panama plant to revive the industry.

In the Old Days of the "Floating Station" Schooner

But Peter's adventures that day were not over. To quote from her invaluable diary:

"On our way back to Government House we met an aged and bent woman who stood still in the middle of the road and literally gibbered at us. When I tried to pass, she caught hold of my hand and shook it with astonishing vigour for one of her decrepit appearance.

"I asked 'Doc' what it was all about, and he told me the poor old thing had walked fifteen miles to see the woman in man's clothing! But she thought she had been deceived because I was wearing unmistakable skirts, and looked too weak to do all the wonderful things she had heard about me.

"The 'Doc' told me further that she must have started before daylight in order to walk that distance, for she was very feeble. I felt terribly embarrassed, as I had neither money nor any trinket with me that I could give her. But, feeling in my pocket, I discovered a little comb I always carry, and also a tube of lip-salve, as my lips dry and crack in a hot climate, and these I handed to her, the latter because it was bright and shiny.

"She evidently realized what the comb was for, but twisted the cosmetic in her poor old fingers and looked puzzled until the top fell off and the creamy-white substance protruded. This she instantly bit off and chewed with evident relish. I do so *hope* I gave satisfaction."

So, aboard the dream ship and away, carrying with us grateful memories of many kindnesses from Niué and its government. May they both prosper as they deserve!

The last farewell we received from this Island called Savage was a fearsome-looking inhabitant on the top-most peak of the reef—I should say terrace—waving a scarlet *si-si*, and yelling blue murder. But we of the dream ship knew better.

THE FRIENDLY ISLANDS AND THE END OF THE DREAM

The island that was savage—Dream's end, and a few realities

CHAPTER XV

The island that was savage—Dream's end, and a few
realities

South, and still south, the dream ship sailed, until the neighbourhood of the "southerly-buster" began to make itself felt in a league-long swell.

We were heading for Tonga Tabu, the southern-most island of the Friendly group where we might turn and sail almost due west for Australia in open sea, instead of picking a precarious and anxious way through the close-meshed network of islets, rocks, and submerged reefs that littered the more direct route.

Even so, we came nearer to disaster amongst these alleged Friendly Islands than we had throughout the entire voyage. Cook so christened them on account of the contrast of his reception here compared with Niué, but we of the dream ship suffered a reversed order of things, and consequently beg to differ with the great navigator.

On the fourth day out from Niué we sighted the group, but decided not to proceed as there are no lights on these outlying reefs, and we had been warned by every island skipper of consequence that a vessel "sights" and "hits" one of them as near simultaneously as no matter. So we hove-to on the tail-end, the very mildly wagging tail-end, of a "southerly-buster," and turned in.

Throughout the night we took it in turns to go on deck at intervals and see that we were not drifting on to anything, and, save for the eternal dirge of the sea that fills the night in the vicinity of any group of South Pacific Islands, all was well. Yet with the sudden sunlight of dawn in these latitudes, we stood aghast at the scene confronting us: on all sides waves, an apparently complete circle of breaking combers, their emerald-green bodies and white-capped heads flashing in the sun. To all appearances we were as effectually trapped as a rat in a cage. Yet how was the thing possible? If there were an inlet into this inferno of reefs there must assuredly be an outlet.

The engine was called upon, and responded nobly. During that day we systematically searched for a loophole of escape, and found none, until toward evening we glided through a passage no more than fifty yards wide, and to our intense relief found that it led to the open sea.

While hove-to the previous night the dream ship must have executed a miracle by drifting into a narrow-necked horseshoe of coral; that was all. And to some it may appear that we were an unconscionable time in finding a way out, but for the benefit of such I would point out that the inside of the horseshoe, as is often the case, was littered with broken reefs, each forming an apparent outlet which on closer inspection proved to be nothing of the sort. In short, I would commend those with a taste for maze-solving to visit the Friendly Islands.

I was not surprised to learn later that local trading craft, equipped with a band of lynx-eyed Kanakas, never sail at night in these waters. Apart from the constant danger of known reefs, others have a knack of appearing and receding in the most uncanny way, so that no chart issued can keep track of them.

In this connection a most enthralling theory engages the attention of the South Sea student. It is his firm belief that what is now the "milky way" of the Pacific was at one time a vast coral and volcanic continent; that it has subsided here, and been upheaved or erupted there, until broken into a myriad fragments, and that the day may still come when Nature will elect to raise them from the deep, welded once more into a mighty whole.

As has been said before (if it were not sufficiently evident without saying at all), I am not a scientist, but the existing indications in support of this theory meet even the casual observer at every turn in the Pacific Ocean to-day. There is a wall on Easter Island, not unlike the great wall of China, but which runs for a short distance and then plunges aimlessly into the sea. Where did it begin? Where did it end? What mighty city did it embrace? On Pitcairn there are the remains of a former and highly advanced civilization. On Lord Howe Island, a mere rock sprouting three thousand feet out of the sea four hundred and eighty miles from the Australian coast, there are sixty different species of land shell, 50 per cent. of which are not to be found anywhere else in the world. How do they come to be on Lord Howe? Land shell cannot swim. In the Carolines, you may look down into the water of lagoons and see the remains—mosaic floors and broken walls—of a submerged city.

So, from east to west, and from north to south, this mighty ocean of the Pacific holds its secrets of forgotten lands and peoples.

As for the dream ship, not content with escape from a coral death-trap, we sailed out, and still out to the open sea, until nothing short of a gale could carry us into danger, and there hove-to again for the night. There was nothing else to be done. What was more, and owing to an oversight attributable to no one but myself, we had no large-scale chart of Tonga Tabu, so that it took us three days of searching and three nights of heaving to before we found the eastern pass through the reef and waited with international code flag flying for the pilot.

Natives in canoe

We could see his station and flagstaff on a sandspit, but no flag in answer to our own. We waited, and continued to wait, while a three-knot current carried us up the ever-narrowing channel to within fifty feet of the coral bar at its end. And then it was that the motor auxiliary that I have so consistently reviled throughout these pages vindicated itself by saving us from certain destruction. It went! Literally inch by inch it fought the current for the hour or more we were obliged to wait on that pilot's pleasure.

I can hear the "expert's" wail of enquiry: "Why not have anchored?" My answer is that I should like to see him try. Is he aware that coral alters all one's preconceived ideas of seamanship? Does he know that although the passage walls were not more than fifty feet from either side of us, the water between was unfathomable; that to put out a kedge was equally hopeless because exposed coral is nothing more than a brittle honeycomb that breaks like pie-crust; that—— But I refuse further enlightenment. Let my imagined critic learn from experience as I was forced to do.

At long last the pilot came, in an outrigger canoe that was swept from under his feet by the current as he clambered aboard. He did not know... He thought our code flag was a burgee, that we were a local trading cutter, that we were almost anything but what we were. There are moments too full for words, and this was one.

The Friendly Islands have a real queen and a consort, and I reported that pilot to both of them, though my plaint merely elicited a charming smile from the one and the suggestion of a whisky-and-soda from the other. It's a way they have in the Islands.

I fear this account of Tonga Tabu will be unsympathetic, and for that reason I would suggest the perusal of several excellent books on the subject. For me it was a place of tragedy, and as such remains with me to this day. My views are jaundiced; let them lie! All I know is that in the island capital of Nukualofa there is a club, and from that club emerged a genial gentleman who, had I known what I know now, would never have set foot aboard the dream ship. He came, he saw, and we repaired to the club.

"Do you want to sell that boat of yours?" he asked me.

"No," said I.

"*Will* you sell her?" he corrected himself.

"Not for what any sane man would care to pay," I told him.

"And what is that, may I ask?"

I named a figure sufficiently preposterous to raise a laugh from most people. But the genial gentleman did not laugh.

"You would take no less?" he suggested bravely.

"Not a cent," said I. "As a matter of fact——"

"I suppose a draft on —— will satisfy you?"

"What's that?" I stammered.

"I'll take her," said the genial gentleman. "I was saying that...."

But I heard no more. I had sold the dream ship!

Confession is said to be good for the soul, but I have not noticed much improvement in the state of my own since making the above statement. Imagine parting for pelf with a home that has conveyed you across twelve thousand miles of ocean. Or, better, try to imagine selling your best friend, and you have some idea of my feelings since the transaction. And there was no going back on it. I have not the moral courage of such deeds. The draft lay on the table before me, I had a pocket full of money, and no ship. I have never been so miserable in my life.

It took me the best part of an hour's aimless wandering over the powdered coral roads of Nukualofa to summon the necessary courage to break the news to the crew of the dream ship, but by the end of that time I had some sort of scheme evolved. Between the Friendlies and Australia there were no islands of particular interest, anyway. We would continue our journey by steamer—it would be a pleasant change—and in New Zealand or Australia I would invest my ill-gotten gains in a far more magnificent vessel than the dream ship.

On this "more magnificent" craft, we would carry out our original programme of cruising up the Queensland coast to the islands of the northwest Pacific, and so home via Java, Colombo, and the Suez Canal, thereby avoiding the monotonous passage between the Friendlies and Australia. Rather clever, I thought. Nevertheless, I prefer to draw a veil over the communication of this brilliant scheme to the rest of the crew. Peter did not speak to me for the rest of the day. I verily believe she hates me, but not a tithe more than I hate myself. It is enough that we took our departure by steamer according to schedule, and without daring to look back on the good ship we had left behind. The heart had gone out of things; the dream was ended.

Or rather it had merged into a nightmare. We proceeded to rub shoulders with a horde of fellow-passengers who no doubt regarded us as unattractive as we regarded them; to consume beef-tea or ice-cream at eleven o'clock, and push lumps of wood about the deck with a stick for want of something better to do.

Is there anything more wearisome than a steamer voyage—after sailing your own ship? You sleep throughout the night instead of breaking the twenty-four hours into the sensible segments of four "on" and eight "off." You are called by a smug-faced steward instead of being gently squeezed or roughly shaken into life by the previous "watch"; and instead of commanding your own destinies at the tiller under the stars, you watch others doing it in brass buttons and electric light from a bridge. You begin to wonder if your tie is straight, if it would be permissible to rid your chafing neck of the unholy contrivance encircling it.

As for your fellow-passengers, they are—to a man, and to a woman—gross from over-indulgence of one form or another—mostly food and drink, and their interests are as far removed from yours as the stars. You begin to see how the average sailor-man feels in "polite society," and your heart goes out to him.

"How's the wind?" Ah, of course, it makes no difference to this smoke-belching machine that bears you at thirteen knots, and according to schedule, toward civilization. See that wave? The big fellow with the curling top! Isn't he twin brother to the one you met in the Caribbean when...

No, no. Give us the "sleepy" twelve-to-four watch, and even a "cooking week" aboard the dream ship that we may be content once more.

Already, we were changed to each other's eye. Oftentimes I stood with Steve on the promenade deck, and his well-known figure, camouflaged at the moment under a natty blue suit and collar and tie complete, would fade and merge like a dissolving view into a brown-skinned, happy savage in towel and sola topi. And as for Peter—she was no longer the Peter we had known for a happy ten-month, but a female slave to every twist and quiff of convention. And it was my doing ... all my doing. Or can I thrust the blame on other shoulders after the fashion of brother Adam? Is it not our women-folk who make convention necessary at all to men who, if they followed natural instincts, would revert to the enviable savage?

At Apia, Samoa, Steve was so heartily tired of his environment that he left the ship. He said he could scent civilization afar, and would have none of it. He had met a military official ashore who had offered him a post in the Government on the strength of his war services, and he had accepted. He would stay there in Samoa until I had found another dream ship, when he would join her on receipt of a cable, and continue with us over the remaining half of the world.

He made this promise with an ironical twinkle of the eye that puzzled me at the time, but which has since been abundantly and painfully accounted for.

He left in a native outrigger canoe, hugging his knees on a pyramid of bananas, while the remainder of "the crew" waved him farewell from the steamer's rail, and turned sadly away. A better mate for any venture calling on the best qualities of a man never breathed. Here's to him, "down under," and may that cable not be long delayed!

THURSDAY ISLAND

Concerning a wild-goose chase, and where it led

CHAPTER XVI

Concerning a wild-goose chase, and where it led

Life for the sad remnants of the dream ship's crew resolved itself into the pursuit of a will-o'-the-wisp.

It was a strange craft that we were after: sufficiently staunch to stand any weather, yet small enough to be handled by a crew of three. The New Zealand seaboard had neither heard of nor seen such a thing. At Auckland and Wellington we were hustled off in launch or car with high hope in our hearts, and shown every manner of contrivance that floats, but there was no choice between hundred-ton schooners and harbour racing machines. New Zealand is a beautiful, over-legislated, intensely earnest little country, but for us it held no dream ship, and we passed on.

Australia was little better. Adelaide, Melbourne, Sydney were visited in turn, and scoured from end to end without producing anything within coo-ee of what we sought. With an "I-told-you-so" glint in her eye, Peter departed on a jaunt to New Guinea, and I continued the search alone, after the fashion of the "last little nigger boy."

Hearing that the Torres Straits pearling luggers were likely craft, I set my teeth and journeyed on a Chinese liner—incidentally one of the most comfortable and well-managed ships it has been my good fortune to encounter—up through the myriad islets of the Queensland barrier reef to Thursday Island.

It is a strange thing on a ten-thousand-ton liner to awake at night to a silence unbroken even by the familiar throbbing of the engines, and to feel the great ship rising and falling on the swell like any cockleshell; to go on deck and find her lying at anchor under a panoply of stars, and apparently in mid-ocean, for there is no sign of land. Yet this is a frequent experience of any passenger traversing the barrier reef. Whether liner or dream ship, it makes no difference to the infinite care necessary in navigating these reef-infested seas.

A young navy of pilots performs the miracle—for miracle it is. After long apprenticeship they learn the exact dimensions of every open stretch of water, and if they leave one side at nightfall, they can tell by the vessel's speed, and to a yard, when they have reached the other, when they anchor until dawn. The farther we progressed up the magnificently rugged coast of Queensland, the more varied became the nature of our passenger list. There were sun-baked pastoralists from the cattle and sheep stations "out back" who owned herds and acreages that would cause the largest Western American rancher to open his eyes. One of them at a recent cattle "muster" had tallied up to half a million head, and he had not finished yet. The possibilities of the "Northern Territory," as it is called, are infinite—if it were not for the bugbear of labour troubles that stalks Australia with a heavier tread than any other country of the world.

Then, there were commercial travellers—not the sleek variety that boards a "flyer" and is on its battle-ground in a matter of hours, but lean, hard-bitten men who take a launch or trading cutter and traverse vast stretches of ocean to the farthermost corners of the Gulf of Carpentaria, sleeping, eating, and having their being for weeks together in a stifling, evil-smelling deck house with native "boys" and their own sample cases for sole company.

Wireless operators, engineers, pearlers, teachers of aboriginal schools, Chinamen, Japanese, all were on their way to this mysterious equatorial land of vast, unexplored spaces.

A great deal has been written about Thursday Island, otherwise known as "T.I.", but, without exception, accounts refer to a more picturesque past when this sun-baked tile on the roof of Australia was the busy headquarters of a pearling fleet manned by "whites" and native "boys"; when hefty schooners were employed as floating stations, where shell was opened and treated at sea under the lynx-eyed supervision of a skipper or mate who claimed the hidden treasure it might contain. To-day, the pearling fleet is manned entirely by Japanese, who work on a prosaic fifty-per-cent. basis, and are entitled to every pearl they find.

But of this, later. There were luggers in the bay, likely-looking craft, the most likely I had seen in all my weary pilgrimage. Was it possible that I was on the verge of being able to look Peter in the eye once more—and send a cable to Samoa?

High Holiday on a "T. I." Beach

High Holiday on a "T.I." Beach

Not five minutes after landing in the corrugated-iron and goat-infested landscape of Thursday Island I was in the shipyards watching an army of Japanese workmen putting the finishing touches to a pearling lugger. Yes, I was told by the manager of the Pearling Company that had commissioned her, I could have a similar craft built for —— (a sum nearly double the seemingly preposterous figure I had received for the dream ship)—and she could be delivered in about a year! Labour, you know, prices of material—everything! Things were not as they used to be on 'T.I.'. Or yes; there were second-hand craft to be picked up, but it stood to reason they would have passed their day, or they would not be sold.

Festival Headdress of Torres Straits Islanders

The Japanese Club

Festival Headdress of Torres Straits Islanders;
The Japanese Club

I boarded twelve in all, and examined them from truck to keelson. In some cases one could scoop the dry-rot out of their timbers in handfuls; in others—— But why continue? In all of them the head-room was practically nil because of their light draught for negotiating reefs and sand-bars, and because the Japanese have no manner of use for head-room. When below, they live, move, and have their being on their heel-supported haunches. It would be necessary for the average Anglo-Saxon to crawl on all fours to escape a permanent crick in the neck and stooped shoulders aboard a pearling lugger.

It was in that hour that I realized my final defeat. Peter and Steve were right—there never would be another dream ship. I resigned myself to the inevitable, and settled down on Thursday Island to await the next southern-bound steamer in two weeks' time. I wandered amidst sweltering corrugated iron and herds of cavorting goats, thinking my own sad and secret thoughts, until taken under the wing of two as bright lads as one could wish to meet. We "batched it," if you please, and I am consequently in a position to state precisely how one may live on T.I. in this year of grace.

Taking it in turns to leave your sagging camp bed a trifle before dawn, you steal forth into the iron-bound forest of the settlement, and stalk your prey. It is a simple process. You offer the most appetizing-looking kid in sight a lump of sugar with one hand, and, seizing its hind leg with the other, smother its cries with a towel. Half an hour later it has been converted over a Primus into something that looks like shoe-leather and tastes like kerosene.

In the alleged "cool" of the evening, you may play lawn tennis. We did, in shorts and a vest, and with diver's-suit rubber an inch thick glued to the soles of our shoes by way of protection against the heat and hardness of the court. In five minutes you are a dripping rag of perspiration, but no matter, it is tennis, and the bright lads could play, though argument across the net seemed their strongest point. One of these resolved itself into a bet as to who would win a game played in diver's helmet and boots respectively. It was put to the test with the utmost gravity, and resulted in a dead heat, the man in the helmet being unable to see through his three glass windows quickly enough to take the ball, and the booted competitor being unable to move.

Such were some of the social amenities of T.I., interspersed with delightful evenings spent with the *haute monde*, consisting of military authorities and owners of pearling fleets, in their charming bungalows situated behind and above the settlement. But for the most part we kept to the beach. It was more interesting—and kids were more plentiful.

As for the industries of this queer little island with a white population of five hundred and a black-and-tan one of unknown dimensions, pearling predominates, as different a form of pearling from that of the Paumotus as can well be imagined. Here machinery is permissible, and with the up-to-date motor compressor keeping up a mechanically uniform and unfailing air supply, great depths are attained, and shell of a prodigious size and lustre obtained.

"I don't know," mused a pearling-lugger owner of my acquaintance; "I'm beginning to think it's the survival of the fittest, after all. The Japs are the best machine divers in the world. They don't seem to put the same value on life that we do, and maybe they're right; I don't know.

"But I can tell you this: they work as no white man would ever work—day and night for two weeks without shutting an eye; then they bring the stuff in, sleep two days and nights on end, and are ready for another two weeks.

"I used to go out with a crew now and then, and I've seen them go down fifty-two fathoms, and be hauled up dead, and another man climb into his suit and be 'down' inside of ten minutes.

"Another little trick they've got is to sail—almost into the wind, mind you, but still sail—towing a diver along the bottom. It saves him having to walk and he covers more ground; but would you like to be in that suit? What happens if it catches on a bit of coral? ...

"I tell you what it is: they come over here on a three-years' indenture—it's the only way we allow them into Australian territory—and during that time they set out to make enough to keep 'em for the rest of their lives. And they do it—because they don't live long anyway after much fifty-two-fathom diving.

"Skin divers? We've got as good here in Torres Straits as any in the world! Twenty fathoms, and three minutes under water in the Paumotus? Well, that's not so bad, but we can beat it with a good abo (aboriginal). Come and see."

I did, and am forced to give the palm to Torres Straits. Our crew was a hotch-potch of mainland aboriginals—Islanders, Malays, and Filipinos—but it was the aboriginal who did the diving, and his performance was every whit as good as, and in some cases better than, that of the Paumotan. But with what different results! Instead of the cleanly pearl-shell, bèche-de-mer or trepang was brought to light, immense brown or black sea slugs that are gutted, impaled on a stick, and cured in a smoke-box amidships. When cooked they make a soup as nutritious and appetizing as turtle, and although China is by far the largest consumer of bèche-de-mer at the present time, it is rapidly gaining favour in Europe.

Pearl diver

The remaining important products of the Coral Sea and its coasts are trochas shell and sandal wood. The first of these is second only to mother-of-pearl for buttons, knife-handles, and what-not; and as for sandalwood, its uses are too familiar to call for mention here. But I am grateful to this externally unlovely but fragrant tree for taking me to the shores of the Gulf of Carpentaria where it grows in profusion, for a stranger, more deserted land— saving always the Galapagos Islands—it would be difficult to find.

You may stand on these shores and look inland over thousands of miles of gently undulating and lightly timbered country, containing not a living soul with the exception of a few bands of ever-wandering and rapidly decreasing aboriginals. Cotton grows here to perfection. What would not grow? There are rivers that Western-American irrigators would smack their lips over, a light but assured rainfall, a rich loam soil, and millions of acres of pasture untouched save by wallaby and kangaroo. Yet we still cry out that the world is over-full.

Some day the entirely admirable bluff of "white Australia" will be called, and these territories of vast possibilities will be inundated by a people able and eager to develop them. It will be unpleasant, but then so are most penalties of degeneration and sloth in this cannibalistic old world of ours.

Back from "the Gulf," we celebrated a successful trip in the approved fashion at one of Thursday Island's numerous and well-known circular bars, presided over by a high priestess who, after three years in New Guinea, favoured the native style of coiffure.

Discussion turned on a race meeting of the morrow. A race meeting on T.I.! Why not? I had forgotten that wherever you find an assembly of more than two Australians, there you will find a race-course of some sort. It appeared that someone had stolen the favourite; nothing less! The horse had been pastured on Friday Island, a few miles distant, and now, a day before the race, it had vanished. The owner, who happened to be present, was telling us just what he was going to do to the culprit when he caught him, but I fear my attention wandered. An aboriginal was standing at my elbow with the most ghastly healed wound encircling his neck that could have been inflicted without decapitation. How the man could have suffered it and remained alive, was beyond my comprehension.

"That," I was told, "is Treacle, the only man who's had his head in a shark's mouth and got it out again. Care for an introduction?"

I did care, and after sundry amenities elicited the following: "Me push; 'im leave go." That was all, delivered with every appearance of delight and pride in the accomplishment. Some of the shark's teeth were still embedded in the fellow's skull. With a vast grin, he will guide your finger to the spot—for sixpence; and for a like amount one is permitted to photograph Treacle the miraculous.

The Australian "abo's" recuperative qualities are equalled only by his inventiveness. Was he not the originator of the boomerang, that most ingenious of weapons? And had he not, before the advent of the white man, instituted certain surgical operations which might, with advantage, be introduced into other lands? For example, the rendering incapable of a degenerate male parent to propagate his species, whereby his race was kept up to the highest standards of physique.

But let these things pass, as relics of barbarism if you will, and there is still a quaint originality in his make-up that shows itself in his speech. Bèche-de-mer, or Pidgin-English, is his tongue for dealing with white folk, and here is some of his vocabulary:

"Trousers belong letter" = Envelope.

"Bokkus belong noise" = Gramaphone, piano, or almost any musical instrument.

"Pull um come; push um go, brother belong tomahawk" = Saw.

"Belly belong me fnuast" = I am hungry.

"What time papa belong you plant um you?" = How old are you?

Some day there will be a dictionary of Pidgin-English. It would make a diverting document.

For a tiny community like that of Thursday Island, the racing on the following day was too commendable to be treated otherwise than seriously. The course was complete with grandstand and "bleacher" seats, totalisator, judge's box, and bar, and was soon thronged with the entire white population of T.I., and most of the coloured. Jockeys wore anything from orthodox "silk" to an undervest, and rode anything on four legs with immense earnestness, and amidst thunderous acclamation. We lost money or won money, as the case might be, but there is no doubt that we enjoyed ourselves.

At the end of a pleasant and instructive fortnight a south-bound steamer, direct from New Guinea, touched at T.I., and as she came alongside, my gaze became fixed on a slight, inconspicuous but vaguely familiar figure standing at the rail.

It was Peter.

There, on T.I.'s rickety jetty, seated on a stack of sandalwood, we talked of many things; but behind all lurked the eternal question, and I was obliged to answer it:

"I'm beat. You're right, both of you. There never will be another dream ship."

But there I was wrong.

ADVICE TO DREAMERS OF DREAM SHIPS

For the prospective dream-ship owner the world over

CHAPTER XVII

For the prospective dream-ship owner the world over

There are more dreamers in the world than I had reckoned on. So much is evident from the snowdrift of letters received from every corner of the world, asking this, that, and the other in connection with the dream ship, until it became a physical impossibility for me to answer them individually.

Here I hope to answer them all, out of sympathy more than anything else, for I know how the dreamer feels; but let me tell him or her this at the outset: unless you are willing to take a chance, your dream will never be realized. To sail away on a dream cruise is an easier thing than to climb out of the rut you are probably in. There may be the most excellent reasons for your remaining in that rut—marriage and family ties, or ill health—but those are the only insurmountable obstacles in the path of any dream merchant worth his salt.

You will notice, no doubt, that penury is not included in this catalogue of obstacles, and the reason of its absence is that penury ought to be an incentive rather than an obstacle. One must work for dream fulfilment as one is obliged to work for anything worth while.

"It's all very well for you to talk," people have said to me more than once, "but you have no ties; and you always have your writing."

If they only knew, neither of these statements is true. To hear them talk one would think I had neither friend nor relation in the world, and that the average writer makes as much money as a plumber. My reply to such folk is: "All right, let's be personal. You have no ties but what you could fling aside for a while without hurting yourself or any one else, for it is a fifty-to-one chance that they are nothing but money-grubbing at best. It has become a habit with you, that is all. You have enough money to buy a car, why not a tight little cruiser, and sail where you will? And if you have not, you could soon make it, for your trade is less precarious than mine.

"No, my friend, you may sit in that chair, and simulate the adventurous spirit beating its wings at the prison bars of Duty, or some such stuff, but what really ails you is that you are in a rut, and afraid to get out; or else your dream has not taken firm enough hold to hoist you out. The latter is a matter of personal temperament, and cannot be helped, but the former is something quite different. It simply means that you lack initiative, dread possible discomfort, and fear the world."

Please do not imagine because I am pointing out the disabilities of the average dreamer that I claim to be exempt myself. I possess them in an all-too-marked degree, but my dream was strong enough to lift me above them, and it was worth it.

I know a man who, at the age of thirty, and while I was working the soul out of myself on cattle and horse ranch, in lumber-camp and salmon-cannery for an average of two dollars a day, bought a decked-in, dug-out canoe for twenty dollars, and with a capital of a like amount went clean up the British Columbia coast. During the summer he sailed, fished, and shot deer, trading his bag with farmers and store-keepers for other commodities that he needed. In the winter, he laid up the canoe, but lived aboard and trapped fur. He was his own man, and he lived. That was his dream, and he accomplished it. And I might have been doing precisely the same thing all those weary years, and come out a good deal better off at the end of them if I had only had the courage of my dream.

For the benefit of the apparent multitude whose dream lies along much the same lines as my own, I must attack the more technical side of the dream cruise, and, before doing so, I want it to be clearly understood that everything I may say in these pages is simply the outcome of my own personal experience. Others have had different and, perhaps, much wider experience, and will no doubt differ with me at every point. But then, after a woman, and a horse, there never was a subject more provocative of dissension than the proper conduct of a ship. So here's to it!

Out of the Deep

The Main Products of Torres Straits. From left to right:—Green Snail (used for buttons). Pearl-Shell (with natural blister in form of an elephant). Trochas (used for buttons, etc.). At back: Beche-de-mer.

Out of the Deep;
The Main Products of Torres Straits. From left to
right:—Green Snail (used for buttons). Pearl-Shell
(with natural blister in form of an elephant).
Trochas (used for buttons, etc.). At back: Beche-de-mer.

The Dream Ship.—The dream ship is my idea of the ideal ocean cruiser to be handled by a crew of three. That is why I bought her, and she cost (second hand) £300 or about $1,500. She was designed as a North Sea pilot cutter by the late Colin Archer, who also designed the *Fram* for Nansen, and was the originator of this type of vessel. She was built at Porsgrund, Norway, in 1908, and I reduced her canvas to make for easy handling by a small and light-weight crew. For this reason she was slow going to windward, but I would not have had her otherwise for one cannot have *everything*—there is bound to be a compromise somewhere—and one does not expect to go round the world "on a wind."

An Islander's Home on T. I.

The Tennis Handicap

An Islander's Home on T.I.;
The Tennis Handicap

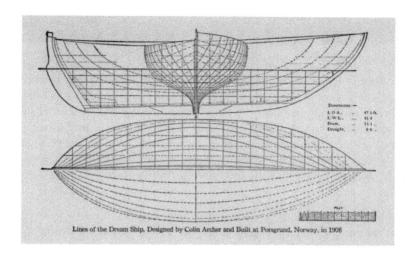

Lines of the Dream Ship, Designed by Colin Archer and Built at Porsgrund, Norway, in 1908

Lines of the Dream Ship,
Designed by Colin Archer and Built
at Porsgrund, Norway, in 1908

Construction.—Her timbers were of pine and her planking of Italian oak, which is admittedly a reversal of the usual order of things, but is easily accounted for by the fact that Norway has plenty of pine (grown on hilltops so that the wind will make it "natural bent" for elbows and knees), but little or no oak; while Italy is oppositely placed, and the two countries trade their woods.

The dream ship was copper-fastened, which made it possible to have her copper-sheathed against the inroads of the tropical cobra worm, and this was an immense saving of labour. With ordinary iron fastenings it is impossible to copper-sheathe because the two metals, when immersed in salt water, set up a galvanic action destructive to both. It must not be imagined, however, that because a boat is iron-fastened she is useless for tropical waters. There is no stronger and better fastening for a boat than galvanized iron, but it entails her under-water body being kept in the best condition by putting her on "the hard" wherever and whenever possible, and paying her up with anti-fouling paint. Most of the Island schooners are iron-fastened, and they last for forty years and longer, if well looked after. If not, they are a honeycomb from worm inside of a year.

The dream ship was of life-boat or "double-ender" build, which means that she was "all ship," and had no counter. Various stems and sterns are recommended by various people, but I have found nothing better than the life-boat.

Rig.—She was cutter rigged, and, always provided that the boom does not extend too far beyond the counter to be easily accessible, it is as handy an arrangement of sail as any other, and admittedly the best for sailing.

I can almost hear the noble army of schooner-, ketch-, and yawl-owners howling their execration at these remarks, but I cannot help it. I have tried most rigs, and come back to the cutter. The howlers will at least admit that she sails as close to the wind as any, and closer than most; and as for facility in handling by the smallest possible crew, we of the dream ship had no trouble on this score, for she would heave-to in a gale under single reef like a duck, and with the wind abeam would go for hours on end with the tiller pegged.

Our main difficulty was that the dream ship was too heavily sparred. The boom was the size of an average mast for a vessel of her tonnage, and the gaff little smaller in proportion.

Next time, we shall have smaller spars, and a top-mast instead of a pole mast. Aboard the dream ship our topsail yard was twenty-three feet long, and many were the anxious moments in lowering it when taking in the topsail during a squall. The topmast does away with any necessity for a yard, and can be lowered to the deck in foul weather, thus also eliminating considerable top-hamper.

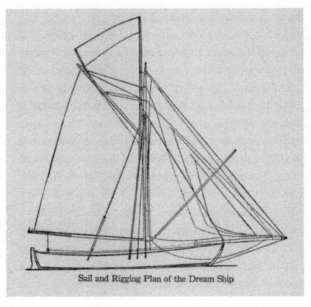

Sail and Rigging Plan of the Dream Ship

Sail and Rigging Plan of the Dream Ship

A hollow topmast and a hollow squaresail yard sound alluring, and have proved themselves efficient in temperate climes, but would they stand the intense heat of, say, the Paumotus? I know they are put to a boiling test for several hours, but what about months? It would be a disconcerting episode, to say the least, if one's spars commenced to open out like a flower in mid-ocean. I am sufficiently generous to allow someone else to make the experiment.

Gear.—The importance of good ground tackle cannot be over-emphasized. Never carry less than one hundred fathoms of sound, galvanized-iron cable, preferably amidships, and see that the anchors have long shanks. We carried three: a skeleton, for dropping for short periods; a medium, for ordinary use; and a large, for holding her in an emergency. We never used any but the medium, and we never dragged anchor, mainly on account of the length of shank.

A winch is better than a capstan for heaving anchor, and if placed abaft the mast, serves also for "swigging" on halyards, or hoisting sail.

As for sails, the dream ship's were all "barked" or tanned after the fisherman style, and there is no doubt that this process prevents rot, especially in the humid tropics. We carried one medium-weight mainsail, a working and a balloon foresail, storm and balloon jibs, and a squaresail, and of these the last was the most generally useful. Again I hear the howlers howling: "Why not a spinnaker?" and my reply is that a squaresail can be used whenever a spinnaker can be used; it is a larger sail, yet infinitely easier to handle.

Our main halyards were of "combination" rope, that is, hemp to all outward appearances, but internally carrying several strands of flexible steel wire. There is nothing stronger, and nothing that will stand the perpetual chafe of a long passage better. Its slight awkwardness in handling compared with ordinary manila is amply atoned for by its durability. I was afraid to use it for peak halyards on account of its inelasticity, but next time it shall be rove throughout, with the exception of the main sheet, which must perforce be of manila.

Wheel- or tiller-steering gear is a matter of taste. Personally, I like to feel the "life" of a ship, and this is better accomplished with a tiller.

Fittings.—A deep-sea cruiser should always be flush-decked, and have an entirely detached, self-emptying cockpit. Coach roofs and immense skylights make for additional headroom below, but during bad weather are an abomination.

We did not carry davits. They look "yachty," but we were not anxious to look that way, and found it far less trouble to haul the thirteen-foot dinghy over the bulwarks with the fore halyards. If one went in for every "fitting" advertised in a yachting catalogue, the deck—which must be kept as clear as possible—would be a scrap-heap of "gadgets."

Brass, too, is a good thing to do without. Again, it looks well, but think of the work it entails, and have painted galvanized-iron instead. There is no reason why a vessel should not look as "ship-shape" with these latter fittings as with all the glinting—and dulling—brasswork in the world.

Good paint is the best wood-preserver there is; for that reason, and several others not unconnected with labour, the dream ship was painted throughout instead of varnished. The decks were painted (pinewood colour), and remained as sound and unscathed at the end of the voyage as they had been at the beginning. Boom and gaff were painted the same colour, hatches and skylights were white, as also were her top sides.

And that is another thing: never have black paint if going to the tropics. The dream ship's cockpit was black, and the helmsman could scarcely bear to touch any part of it with his naked hand, though the white ship's rail was comparatively cool. The mere thought of black top sides in the neighbourhood of the Paumotus causes me to break into a profuse perspiration to this day.

Down below, the two prime factors are ventilation and light. In order to secure the first of these, the dream ship's internal arrangements were of the simplest. There were no separate staterooms, which confine space and are difficult to air. She was open from end to end, save for the bulkheads, each containing a comprehensive doorway, so that the for'ard hatch could be opened and a current of air pass clean through the ship.

As for light, the interior decoration was white enamel, which reflects every gleam from the skylights.

The engine-room was a problem, until we decided—very rightly, as we discovered later—to sacrifice some living space in order to have a roomy "chamber of horrors." It is far more satisfactory to be tortured in a palace than in a pill-box. It leaves adequate space for the expression of feeling.

Because his ship is essentially a sailing vessel, the present-day owner too often tucks his engine away anywhere. It does not do. Some time or other, when the necessary atrocity is engaged in saving life, as ours did on more than one occasion, a vital part of the machinery is found to be out of reach, or so difficult to get at that invaluable time is lost.

As regards cooking and artificial lighting, we had three Primus stoves and an oven on gimbals, over which we contrived to render food eatable, and ordinary swinging lamps. There are those, I know, who prefer electric light on account of its comparative coolness, and to such I would say:

"Enterprising fellow! You like dynamos and fiddling with 'gadgets' generally. Very well." Personally, I am a coward in this department.

Ballast.—There is something peculiarly unattractive about ballast. One sees nothing for many laborious hours spent upon it, and it takes up valuable space. But it must not be forgotten that on its correct distribution the whole stability of a vessel depends. Whether lead, pig-iron, or stone, according to purse, for a cruise anywhere in the neighbourhood of coral, it must be *inside*, and immovable. The reasons for these stipulations are obvious, but too often cruising yachts do not return, and it is not always a matter of a lee shore, broaching to, or being pooped; but ballast.

An excellent plan is to have it cemented in, for this also ensures a clean bilge, but if this is done, the owner would be well advised to have the vessel's timbers surveyed first and a certificate of soundness given, because before now cement has been used for nothing less than hiding rotten timbers.

Palm trees

Auxiliary Engines.—There is no doubt that an auxiliary engine for a deep-sea cruiser is well-nigh indispensable. It may be used but twice in a passage of four thousand miles, as ours was—once for getting out of harbour and once for getting in. But what of the countless contingencies that may arise, such as lee shores, narrow waters, contrary currents and calms, when without power a vessel is helpless?

The heavy-duty, comparatively slow-revolutioned, kerosene-burning type is the best. It may be more cumbersome, and make more noise than the natty little launch engine, but it is infinitely more reliable. A thirteen-horsepower drove the dream ship at four knots through calm water, so one's own particular fancy may be selected on that basis. Each has his own idea as to motor marine engines, and all I can do here is to extend to the engineer my good wishes—and sincerest sympathies.

Deep-Sea Cruising.—The inevitable remark that greets the deep-sea cruiser in small craft on completing a passage is: "Fancy coming all this way in that little thing!" And if the speaker only knew it, his remark is an insult to the owner. There is no reason in the world why a staunch, seaworthy craft of not less than forty-one feet on the waterline should not continue to circumnavigate the globe indefinitely, and with every whit as much safety as a ten-thousand-ton liner. The forty-one-footer goes to the top of every wave; the ten-thousand-tonner rests upon two or more; that is the sole difference.

Before leaving England, "know-alls" were good enough to point out to me that it was a silly game at best; that I was risking my precious life for no particular purpose, and that I should never get where I wanted to, anyway. As for taking one's sister, it was nothing short of murder.

When I returned, the self-same people, chatting over a club "port" between races, agreed that there was, after all, nothing in it. Was not deep-sea cruising in fair-weather latitudes safer than coastal navigation in our pestiferous home waters?

With this latter argument I entirely agree, and would point out that I never held any other view. Moreover, we made the cruise because we wanted to, and not because it was a safe or daring thing to do.

Where to find a Dream Ship.—This, as I think has been sufficiently demonstrated in the foregoing pages, is the most difficult question of all to answer at the present time.

I have given here the design and sail plan of my dream ship, and if it meets with your approval sufficiently to impel you to have a replica, and if you are willing and able to spend in the neighbourhood of £2,500 or about $12,500, I can only suggest going to Porsgrund, Norway, or better still Randers, Denmark (where her timbers could be of Danish oak), and have her built. For this particular type of boat, Scandinavia cannot be equalled, let alone beaten. But in these days, building boats is a pastime for millionaires only.

From this giddy pinnacle of affluence we fall to the next best thing, which is a second-hand boat as like the dream ship in seaworthiness and handiness as it is possible to procure, and that is what I have been searching for ever since the dream cruise ended. There are no more pilot boats of the dream-ship type being built in Norway. Steam has dethroned them, and those still in use are either too old to buy or too invaluable to sell. So, we are reduced to the inevitable compromise, and personally, I think I have found it in an English, Bristol Channel Pilot cutter, for which I paid £450 or, at par, about $2,250.

Yes, I have another dream ship. I have notified Peter. I have cabled to Samoa. Next time....

But that is another dream.

THE END

APPENDIX*

State of Affairs Aboard the Ship—Contents of her Larder—Length of South Seamen's Voyages—Account of a Flying Whale-man—Determination to Leave the Vessel—The Bay of Nukuheva—The Typees—Invasion of their Valley by Porter—Reflections—Glen of Tior—Interview Between the Old King and the French Admiral.

*From "Typee" by Herman Melville, copyright 1892 by Elizabeth S. Melville. Reprinted by permission of The Page Company, publishers of the works of Herman Melville, as follows: Typee, Omoo, Moby Dick, White Jacket

Our ship had not been many days in the harbour of Nukuheva before I came to the determination of leaving her. That my reasons for resolving to take this step were numerous and weighty, may be inferred from the fact that I chose rather to risk my fortunes among the savages of the island, than to endure another voyage on board the *Dolly*. To use the concise, point-blank phrase of the sailors, I had made up my mind to "run away." Now, as a meaning is generally attached to these two words no way flattering to the individual to whom they are applied, it behooves me, for the sake of my own character, to offer some explanation of my conduct.

When I entered on board the *Dolly*, I signed, as a matter of course, the ship's articles, thereby voluntarily engaging, and legally binding myself to serve in a certain capacity for the period of the voyage; and, special considerations apart, I was of course bound to fulfil the agreement. But in all contracts, if one party fail to perform his share of the compact, is not the other virtually absolved from his liability? Who is there who will not answer in the affirmative?

Having settled the principle, then, let me apply it to the particular case in question. In numberless instances had not only, the implied but the specified conditions of the articles been violated on the part of the ship in which I served. The usage on board of her was tyrannical; the sick had been inhumanly neglected; the provisions had been doled out in scanty allowance; and her cruises were unreasonably protracted. The captain was the author of these abuses; it was in vain to think that he would either remedy them, or alter his conduct, which was arbitrary and violent in the extreme. His prompt reply to all complaints and remonstrances was—the butt-end of a hand-spike, so convincingly administered as effectually to silence the aggrieved party.

To whom could we apply for redress? We had left both law and equity on the other side of the Cape; and unfortunately, with a very few exceptions, our crew was composed of a parcel of dastardly and mean-spirited wretches, divided among themselves, and only united in enduring without resistance the unmitigated tyranny of the captain. It would have been mere madness for any two or three of the number, unassisted by the rest, to attempt making a stand against his ill-usage. They would only have called down upon themselves the particular vengeance of this "Lord of the Plank," and subjected their shipmates to additional hardships.

But, after all, these things could have been endured awhile, had we entertained the hope of being speedily delivered from them by the due completion of the term of our servitude. But what a dismal prospect awaited us in this quarter! The longevity of Cape Horn whaling voyages is proverbial, frequently extending over a period of four or five years.

Some long-haired, bare-necked youths, who, forced by the united influences of Captain Marryat and hard times, embark at Nantucket for a pleasure excursion to the Pacific, and whose anxious mothers provide them with bottled milk for the occasion, oftentimes return very respectable middle-aged gentlemen.

The very preparations made for one of these expeditions are enough to frighten one. As the vessel carries out no cargo, her hold is filled with provisions for her own consumption. The owners, who officiate as caterers for the voyage, supply the larder with an abundance of dainties. Delicate morsels of beef and pork, cut on scientific principles from every part of the animal, and of all conceivable shapes and sizes, are carefully packed in salt, and stored away in barrels; affording a never-ending variety in their different degrees of toughness, and in the peculiarities of their saline properties. Choice old water, too, decanted into stout six-barrel casks, and two pints of which are allowed every day to each soul on board; together with ample store of sea-bread, previously reduced to a state of petrifaction, with a view to preserve it either from decay or consumption in the ordinary mode, are likewise provided for the nourishment and gastronomic enjoyment of the crew.

But not to speak of the quality of these articles of sailors' fare, the abundance in which they are put on board a whaling vessel is almost incredible. Oftentimes, when we had occasion to break out in the hold, and I beheld the successive tiers of casks and barrels, whose contents were all destined to be consumed in due course by the ship's company, my heart sank within me.

Although, as a general case, a ship unlucky in falling in with whales continues to cruise after them until she has barely sufficient provisions remaining to take her home, turning round then quietly and making the best of her way to her friends, yet there are instances when even this natural obstacle to the further prosecution of the voyage is overcome by headstrong captains, who, bartering the fruits of their hard-earned toils for a new supply of provisions in some of the ports of Chili or Peru, begin the voyage afresh, with unabated zeal and perseverance. It is in vain that the owners write urgent letters to him to sail for home, and for their sake to bring back the ship, since it appears he can put nothing in her. Not he. He has registered a vow; he will fill his vessel with good sperm oil, or failing to do so, never again strike Yankee soundings.

I heard of one whaler, which after many years' absence was given up for lost. The last that had been heard of her was a shadowy report of her having touched at some of those unstable islands in the far Pacific, whose eccentric wanderings are carefully noted in each new edition of the South Sea charts. After a long interval, however, the *Perseverance*—for that was her name—was spoken somewhere in the vicinity of the ends of the earth, cruising along as leisurely as ever, her sails all bepatched and bequilted with rope-yarns, her spars fished with old pipe stores, and her rigging knotted and spliced in every possible direction. Her crew was composed of some twenty venerable Greenwich-pensioner-looking old salts, who just managed to hobble about deck. The ends of all the running ropes, with the exception of the signal halyards and poop-down-haul, were rove through snatch-blocks, and led to the capstan or windlass, so that not a yard was braced or a sail set without the assistance of machinery.

Her hull was incrusted with barnacles, which completely encased her. Three pet sharks followed in her wake, and every day came alongside to regale themselves from the contents of the cook's bucket, which were pitched over to them. A vast shoal of bonetas and albicores always kept her company.

Such was the account I heard of this vessel, and the remembrance of it always haunted me; what eventually became of her I never learned; at any rate, she never reached home, and I suppose she is still regularly tacking twice in the twenty-four hours somewhere off Desolate Island, or the Devil's-Tail Peak.

Having said thus much touching the usual length of these voyages, when I inform the reader that ours had as it were just commenced, we being only fifteen months out, and even at that time hailed as a late arrival and boarded for news, he will readily perceive that there was little to encourage one in looking forward to the future, especially as I had always had a presentiment that we should make an unfortunate voyage, and our experience so far had justified the expectation.

I may here state, and on my faith as an honest man, that though more than three years have elapsed since I left this same identical vessel, she still continues in the Pacific; and but a few days since I saw her reported in the papers as having touched at the Sandwich Islands, previous to going on the coast of Japan.

But to return to my narrative. Placed in these circumstances then, with no prospect of matters mending if I remained aboard the *Dolly*, I at once made up my mind to leave her: to be sure it was rather an inglorious thing to steal away privily from those at whose hands I had received wrongs and outrages that I could not resent; but how was such a course to be avoided when it was the only alternative left me? Having made up my mind, I proceeded to acquire all the information I could obtain relating to the island and its inhabitants, with a view of shaping my plans of escape accordingly. The result of these inquiries I will now state, in order that the ensuing narrative may be the better understood.

The bay of Nukuheva, in which we were then lying, is an expanse of water not unlike in figure the space included within the limits of a horse-shoe. It is, perhaps, nine miles in circumference. You approach it from the sea by a narrow entrance, flanked on either side by two small twin islets which soar conically to the height of some five hundred feet. From these the shore recedes on both hands, and describes a deep semicircle.

From the verge of the water the land rises uniformly on all sides, with green and sloping acclivities, until from gently rolling hillsides and moderate elevations it insensibly swells into lofty and majestic heights, whose blue outlines ranged all around, close in the view. The beautiful aspect of the shore is heightened by deep and romantic glens, which come down to it at almost equal distances, all apparently radiating from a common centre, and the upper extremities of which are lost to the eye beneath the shadow of the mountains. Down each of these little valleys flows a clear stream, here and there assuming the form of a slender cascade, then stealing invisibly along until it bursts upon the sight again in larger and more noisy waterfalls, and at last demurely wanders along to the sea.

The houses of the natives, constructed of the yellow bamboo, tastefully twisted together in a kind of wickerwork, and thatched with the long tapering leaves of the palmetto, are scattered irregularly along these valleys beneath the shady branches of the cocoanut trees.

Nothing can exceed the imposing scenery of this bay. Viewed from our ship as she lay at anchor in the middle of the harbour, it presented the appearance of a vast natural amphitheatre in decay, and overgrown with vines, the deep glens that furrowed its sides appearing like enormous fissures caused by the ravages of time. Very often when lost in admiration at its beauty I have experienced a pang of regret that a scene so enchanting should be hidden from the world in these remote seas, and seldom meet the eyes of devoted lovers of nature.

Besides this bay the shores of the island are indented by several other extensive inlets, into which descend broad and verdant valleys. These are inhabited by as many distinct tribes of savages, who, although speaking kindred dialects of a common language, and having the same religion and laws, have from time immemorial waged hereditary warfare against each other. The intervening mountains, generally two or three thousand feet above the level of the sea, geographically define the territories of each of these hostile tribes, who never cross them, save on some expedition of war or plunder. Immediately adjacent to Nukuheva, and only separated from it by the mountains seen from the harbour, lies the lovely valley of Happar, whose inmates cherish the most friendly relations with the inhabitants of Nukuheva. On the other side of Happar, and closely adjoining it, is the magnificent valley of the dreaded Typees, the unappeasable enemies of both these tribes.

These celebrated warriors appear to inspire the other islanders with unspeakable terrors. Their very name is a frightful one; for the word "Typee" in the Marquesan dialect signifies a lover of human flesh. It is rather singular that the title should have been bestowed upon them exclusively, inasmuch as the natives of all this group are irreclaimable cannibals. The name may, perhaps, have been given to denote the peculiar ferocity of this clan, and to convey a special stigma along with it.

These same Typees enjoy a prodigious notoriety all over the islands. The natives of Nukuheva would frequently recount in pantomime to our ship's company their terrible feats, and would show the marks of wounds they had received in desperate encounters with them. When ashore they would try to frighten us by pointing to one of their own number, and calling him a Typee, manifesting no little surprise that we did not take to our heels at so terrible an announcement. It was quite amusing, too, to see with what earnestness they disclaimed all cannibal propensities on their own part, while they denounced their enemies—the Typees—as inveterate gormandizers of human flesh; but this is a peculiarity to which I shall hereafter have occasion to allude.

Although I was convinced that the inhabitants of our bay were as arrant cannibals as any of the other tribes on the island, still I could not but feel a particular and most unqualified repugnance to the aforesaid Typees. Even before visiting the Marquesas, I had heard from men who had touched at the group on former voyages some revolting stories in connection with these savages; and fresh in my remembrance was the adventure of the master of the *Katherine*, who only a few months previous, imprudently venturing into this bay in an armed boat for the purpose of barter, was seized by the natives, carried back a little distance into this valley, and was saved from a cruel death only by the intervention of a young girl, who facilitated his escape by night along the beach to Nukuheva.

I had heard, too, of an English vessel that many years ago, after a weary cruise, sought to enter the bay of Nukuheva, and arriving within two or three miles of the land, was met by a large canoe filled with natives, who offered to lead the way to the place of their destination. The captain, unacquainted with the localities of the island, joyfully acceded to the proposition—the canoe paddled on, and the ship followed. She was soon conducted to a beautiful inlet, and dropped her anchor in its waters beneath the shadows of the lofty shore. That same night the perfidious Typees, who had thus inveigled her into their fatal bay, flocked aboard the doomed vessel by hundreds, and at a given signal murdered every soul on board.

I shall never forget the observation of one of our crew as we were passing slowly by the entrance of this bay on our way to Nukuheva. As we stood gazing over the side at the verdant headlands, Ned, pointing with his hand in the direction of the treacherous valley, exclaimed, "There—there's Typee. Oh, the bloody cannibals, what a meal they'd make of us if we were to take it into our heads to land! but they say they don't like sailor's flesh, it's too salt. I say, maty, how should you like to be shoved ashore there, eh?" I little thought, as I shuddered at the question, that in the space of a few weeks I should actually be a captive in that self-same valley.

The French, although they had gone through the ceremony of hoisting their colours for a few hours at all the principal places of the group, had not as yet visited the bay of Typee, anticipating a fierce resistance on the part of the savages there, which for the present at least they wished to avoid. Perhaps they were not a little influenced in the adoption of this unusual policy from a recollection of the warlike reception given by the Typees to the forces of Captain Porter, about the year 1814, when that brave and accomplished officer endeavoured to subjugate the clan merely to gratify the mortal hatred of his allies the Nukuhevas and Happars.

On that occasion I have been told that a considerable detachment of sailors and marines from the frigate *Essex*, accompanied by at least two thousand warriors of Happar and Nukuheva, landed in boats and canoes at the head of the bay, and after penetrating a little distance into the valley, met with the stoutest resistance from its inmates. Valiantly, although with much loss, the Typees disputed every inch of ground, and after some hard fighting obliged the assailants to retreat and abandon their design of conquest.

The invaders, on their march back to the sea, consoled themselves for their repulse by setting fire to every house and temple on their route; and a long line of smoking ruins defaced the once-smiling bosom of the valley, and proclaimed to its pagan inhabitants the spirit that reigned in the breasts of Christian soldiers. Who can wonder at the deadly hatred of the Typees to all foreigners after such unprovoked atrocities?

Thus it is that they whom we denominate "savages" are made to deserve the title. When the inhabitants of some sequestered island first descry the "big canoe" of the European rolling through the blue waters toward their shores, they rush down to the beach in crowds, and with open arms stand ready to embrace the strangers. Fatal embrace! They fold to their bosoms the vipers whose sting is destined to poison all their joys; and the instinctive feeling of love within their breasts is soon converted into the bitterest hate.

The enormities perpetrated in the South Seas upon some of the inoffensive islanders well-nigh pass belief. These things are seldom proclaimed at home; they happen at the very ends of the earth; they are done in a corner, and there are none to reveal them. But there is, nevertheless, many a petty trader that has navigated the Pacific, whose course from island to island might be traced by a series of cold-blooded robberies, kidnappings, and murders, the iniquity of which might be considered almost sufficient to sink her guilty timbers to the bottom of the sea.

Sometimes vague accounts of such things reach our firesides, and we coolly censure them as wrong, impolitic, needlessly severe, and dangerous to the crews of other vessels. How different is our tone when we read the highly wrought description of the massacre of the crew of the *Hobomak* by the Feejees! how we sympathize for the unhappy victims, and with what horror do we regard the diabolical heathens, who, after all, have but avenged the unprovoked injuries which they have received! We breathe nothing but vengeance, and equip armed vessels to traverse thousands of miles of ocean in order to execute summary punishment upon the offenders. On arriving at their destination, they burn, slaughter, and destroy, according to the tenor of written instructions, and sailing away from the scene of devastation, call upon all Christendom to applaud their courage and their justice.

How often is the term "savages" incorrectly applied! None really deserving of it were ever yet discovered by voyagers or by travellers. They have discovered heathens and barbarians, whom by horrible cruelties they have exasperated into savages. It may be asserted, without fear of contradiction, that in all the cases of outrages committed by Polynesians, Europeans have at some time or other been the aggressors, and that the cruel and bloodthirsty disposition of some of the islanders is mainly to be ascribed to the influence of such examples.

But to return. Owing to the mutual hostilities of the different tribes I have mentioned, the mountainous tracts which separate their respective territories remain altogether uninhabited; the natives invariably dwelling in the depths of the valleys, with a view of securing themselves from the predatory incursions of their enemies, who often lurk along their borders, ready to cut off any imprudent straggler, or make a descent upon the inmates of some sequestered habitation. I several times met with very aged men, who from this cause had never passed the confines of their native vale, some of them having never even ascended midway up the mountains in the whole course of their lives, and who, accordingly, had little idea of the appearance of any other part of the island, the whole of which is not perhaps more than sixty miles in circuit. The little space in which some of these clans pass away their days would seem almost incredible.

The glen of Tior will furnish a curious illustration of this. The inhabited part is not more than four miles in length, and varies in breadth from half a mile to less than a quarter. The rocky vine-clad cliffs on one side tower almost perpendicularly from their base to the height of at least fifteen hundred feet; while across the vale—in striking contrast to the scenery opposite—grass-grown elevations rise one above another in blooming terraces. Hemmed in by these stupendous barriers, the valley would be altogether shut out from the rest of the world, were it not that it is accessible from the sea at one end and by a narrow defile at the other.

The impression produced upon my mind, when I first visited this beautiful glen, will never be obliterated.

I had come from Nukuheva by water in the ship's boat, and when we entered the bay of Tior it was high noon. The heat had been intense, as we had been floating upon the long smooth swell of the ocean, for there was but little wind. The sun's rays had expended all their fury upon us; and to add to our discomfort, we had omitted to supply ourselves with water previous to starting. What with heat and thirst together, I became so impatient to get ashore, that when at last we glided toward it, I stood up in the bow of the boat ready for a spring. As she shot two-thirds of her length high upon the beach, propelled by three or four strong strokes of the oars, I leaped among a parcel of juvenile savages, who stood prepared to give us a kind reception; and with them at my heels, yelling like so many imps, I rushed forward across the open ground in the vicinity of the sea, and plunged, diver fashion, into the recesses of the first grove that offered.

What a delightful sensation did I experience! I felt as if floating in some new element, while all sorts of gurgling, trickling, liquid sounds fell upon my ear. People may say what they will about the refreshing influences of a cold-water bath, but commend me, when in a perspiration, to the shade baths of Tior, beneath the cocoanut trees, and amidst the cool delightful atmosphere which surrounds them.

How shall I describe the scenery that met my eye, as I looked out from this verdant recess! The narrow valley, with its steep and close adjoining sides draperied with vines, and arched overhead with a fretwork of interlacing boughs, nearly hidden from view by masses of leafy verdure, seemed from where I stood like an immense arbour disclosing its vista to the eye, whilst as I advanced it insensibly widened into the loveliest vale eye ever beheld.

It so happened that the very day I was in Tior the French admiral, attended by all the boats of his squadron, came down in state from Nukuheva to take formal possession of the place. He remained in the valley about two hours, during which time he had a ceremonious interview with the king. The patriarch-sovereign of Tior was a man very far advanced in years; but though age had bowed his form and rendered him almost decrepit, his gigantic frame retained all its original magnitude and grandeur of appearance. He advanced slowly and with evident pain, assisting his tottering steps with the heavy war-spear he held in his hand, and attended by a group of gray-bearded chiefs, on one of whom he occasionally leaned for support. The admiral came forward with head uncovered and extended hand, while the old king saluted him by a stately flourish of his weapon. The next moment they stood side by side, these two extremes in the social scale—the polished, splendid Frenchman, and the poor tattooed savage. They were both tall and noble-looking men; but in other respects how strikingly contrasted! Du Petit Thouars exhibited upon his person all the paraphernalia of his naval rank. He wore a richly decorated admiral's frock-coat, a laced *chapeau bras*, and upon his breast were a variety of ribbons and orders; while the simple islander, with the exception of a slight cincture about his loins, appeared in all the nakedness of nature.

At what immeasurable distance, thought I, are these two beings removed from each other. In the one is shown the result of long centuries of progressive civilization and refinement, which have gradually converted the mere creature into the semblance of all that is elevated and grand; while the other, after the lapse of the same period, has not advanced one step in the career of improvement. "Yet, after all," quoth I to myself, "insensible as he is to a thousand wants, and removed from harassing cares, may not the savage be the happier man of the two?" Such were the thoughts that arose in my mind as I gazed upon the novel spectacle before me. In truth, it was an impressive one, and little likely to be effaced. I can recall even now with vivid distinctness every feature of the scene. The umbrageous shades where the interview took place, the glorious tropical vegetation around, the picturesque grouping of the mingled throng of soldiery and natives, and even the golden-hued bunch of bananas that I held in my hand at the time, and of which I occasionally partook while making the aforesaid philosophical reflections.